HOW to USE

America Online® 5

SAMS

A Division of Macmillan USA
201 West 103rd Street
Indianapolis, Indiana 46290

Deborah Craig

Visually in Full Color

How to Use America Online® 5

International Standard Book Number: 0-672-31802-4

Library of Congress Catalog Card Number: **99-65593**

Printed in the United States of America

First Printing: January 2000

03   02   01   00   4   3   2   1

Acquisitions Editor
Elizabeth Brown

Development Editor
Alice Martina Smith

Managing Editor
Charlotte Clapp

Project Editor
Christina Smith

Copy Editor
Alice Martina Smith

Indexer
Deborah Hittel

Proofreader
Tony Reitz

Technical Editor
Dennis Teague

Team Coordinator
Amy Patton

Interior Designers
Nathan Clement
Ruth Lewis

Cover Designers
Aren Howell
Nathan Clement

Copy Writer
Eric Borgert

Production
Stacy DeRome
Dan Harris
Tim Osborn
Mark Walchle

Contents at a Glance

Contents

About the Author

Deborah Craig has been writing and editing books about computers for more than ten years. She has written more than a dozen books on subjects including Excel, Word for Windows, Access, CorelDRAW, FrontPage, and America Online. In her rare spare moments, she plays drums for the Monday Night Band and takes hard-to-decipher photographs with her 1940s Rolliflex camera. She lives in Oakland, California, with her two trusty dogs and one perfidious kitty.

Dedication

For my mother and father.

Acknowledgements

Every book project is a collaborative effort, typically with a large crew of people bailing out the author in various capacities along the way. This time around, as usual, I'm indebted to a long list of people. At Macmillan, acquisitions editor **Elizabeth Brown** got this project off on the right track and deftly helped keep it there. **Amy Patton** worked behind the scenes to keep the wheels running smoothly. **Dennis Teague** provided an insightful technical review. **Alice Martina Smith** did an outstanding job on the development edit, catching innumerable errors and inconsistencies both large and small—all with such good graces that I never felt I had fouled up too glaringly.

Plenty of nonpublishing friends helped me through the often arduous process of producing this book. **Carol DeArment** provided unswerving moral support and a steady supply of fantastic audio tapes—all *pro bono*. The two of us also made several special excursions to Capitola to play music with the truly incomparable jazz pianist **Jessica Williams**. Thanks to Jessica and **Elaine Arc** for welcoming us into their home, and to Jessica for sharing some of the most inspirational music I've heard in almost a lifetime of listening. On a more cacophonous musical note, the **Monday Night Band** faithfully continues to spawn both wondrous and baffling forms of sonic expression. Special thanks to **Greg Goodman**, **Joe Sabella**, **Terry Rolleri**, **George Cremaschi**, and many other distinguished musical guests too numerous to mention.

The **Biow/Shivers/Pecore Family** were a crackerjack marathon support team—fetching me at the airport uncomplainingly, dropping me off at the race at an ungodly hour, collecting me at the finish line, and icing my legs in the aftermath to ensure that I could walk again. Thanks also to the **East Bay Frontrunners** for so many miles of encouragement.

Martha Barrera wins this year's housemate of the year award and has a gift for showing up with chocolate just when you think you can go no further. **Susan Colson** came through in a pinch every time—all while juggling motherhood and a schedule even more maniacal than my own. **Cassie Scott** is a faithful friend and an expert listener. **Marge Jamison**, who has known me longer than just about anyone else, stays helpfully close from a long distance. And **Johanna Clark**, **Rebecca Black**, **Suzanne Slyman**, and **Patricia Robertson** doctored me up in all the right ways at all the right moments.

My resident canines, **Moki** and **Pogo**, continue to provide shining examples of unwavering loyalty, optimism, and huge joy in the small pleasures of life.

Tell Us What You Think!

As the reader of this book, *you* are our most important critic and commentator. We value your opinion and want to know what we're doing right, what we could do better, what areas you'd like to see us publish in, and any other words of wisdom you're willing to pass our way.

You can fax, email, or write directly to let me know what you did or didn't like about this book—as well as what we can do to make our books stronger.

Please note that I cannot help you with technical problems related to the topic of this book, and that because of the high volume of mail I receive, I might not be able to reply to every message.

When you write, please be sure to include this book's title and author as well as your name and phone or fax number. I will carefully review your comments and share them with the author and editors who worked on the book.

Fax: 317-581-4770

Email: internet_sams@mcp.com

Mail: Mark Taber
Associate Publisher
Sams Publishing
201 West 103rd Street
Indianapolis, IN 46290 USA

How To Use This Book

The Complete Visual Reference

Each chapter of this book is made up of a series of short, instructional tasks, designed to help you understand all the information that you need to get the most out of America Online 5.

Click: Click the left mouse button once.

Double-click: Click the left mouse button twice in rapid succession.

Right-click: Click the right mouse button once.

Pointer Arrow: Highlights an item onscreen that you need to point to or focus on in the step or task.

Selection: Highlights the area onscreen discussed in the step or task.

Click and Type: Click once where indicated and begin typing to enter your text or data.

Click & Drag

Release

Drag & drop: Position the mouse pointer over the object, click and hold the left mouse button, drag the object to its new location, and release the mouse button.

Key icons: Clearly indicate which key combinations to use.

Each task includes a series of easy-to-understand steps designed to guide you through the procedure.

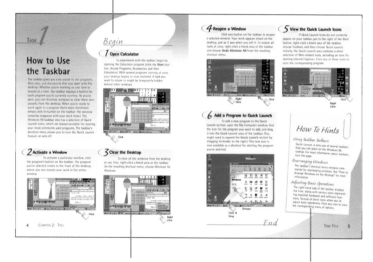

Each step is fully illustrated to show you how it looks onscreen.

Extra hints that tell you how to accomplish a goal are provided in most tasks.

Each task includes a series of easy-to-understand steps designed to guide you through the procedure.

Each step is fully illustrated to show you how it looks onscreen.

Extra hints that tell you how to accomplish a goal are provided in most tasks.

Screen elements (such as menus, icons, windows, and so on), as well as things you select, appear in **boldface type**. Words in *italic* are defined in the glossary. Information you type is in a special font.

Introduction

America Online, fondly known as AOL, is the world's largest online service. Many other online services offer the same basic array of features, but each does so with a unique emphasis. In today's market, all online services provide access to the Internet and the World Wide Web. In addition, they serve up content of their own—ranging from chat rooms in which you can carry on real-time conversations to topic areas (called *channels* in AOL) where you can hunt for information on specific subjects. Some services focus on the needs of businesses and experienced computer users. Others, America Online included, tend to cater to ordinary mortals, serving more personal needs.

Typically, the specialized features and information offered by an online service are available only to members of the service. Unlike AOL, some service providers simply enable you to access the Internet without providing extra content on top of that; such services are called *Internet service providers* or *ISPs*.

America Online consists of two basic components: the service and the communications software. To keep things straight, this book refers to the service, or the service and software collectively, as *America Online*. When talking specifically about the software, this book uses the term *America Online 5.0 for Windows*.

America Online (the service) is headquartered in Vienna, Virginia, just outside Washington, D.C. The AOL service is a set of computers that contains massive quantities of data available for AOL members to use. This information is constantly updated so that you always get the most recent details when you check something, such as a news report.

America Online 5.0 for Windows (the software) needs to reside on the hard disk of any computer that will be connecting to America Online. Software tells computers what to do, and computers can be set up to run all types of software—word processing programs, spreadsheets, databases, and games, to name just a few. The America Online for Windows software tells your computer how to connect to America Online. The tasks in Part 1 of this book explain how to set up America Online 5.0 for Windows on your computer. (There's a chance that America Online for Windows is already installed on your computer. If so, you should see an America Online desktop icon or menu item, and you won't have to go through the installation task.)

Note that this book is specifically written for use with America Online for Windows version 5.0. Unless you have the correct version of the software, you can't be sure that everything you read in this book applies to you. To check your version number (if the software is already installed), choose **About America Online** from the **Help** menu. If you're installing from a CD or downloading the software from America Online's Web site, make sure that you're getting version 5.0.

As the name implies, the America Online 5.0 for Windows software is based on Microsoft Windows, a program that controls, among other things, the "look" of your computer screen. The America Online 5.0 for Windows interface (that is, the way you give commands to the software and receive information from it) is similar to that of other Windows-based software, including some you may already know how to use. (If you feel shaky about certain basic Windows concepts and skills, such as what it means to *drag* with your mouse and how to use menus and dialog boxes, it wouldn't be a bad idea to consult a basic book on Windows.)

To make the connection between your computer and the ones in Virginia, you most likely use ordinary telephone lines. Because telephone lines are designed for human voices rather than computer information, your computer must have a special piece of equipment called a *modem* (short for *modulator/demodulator*) to translate the computer information traveling to and from your computer. Your modem may be internal (hidden inside your computer's main case) or external (a small box sitting outside the case). If you're not sure whether you have a modem, look in the documentation you received with your computer, check with the vendor who sold you your computer, or ask a computer-savvy friend. (New computers almost invariably come equipped with an internal modem.) If you have only a single phone line, keep in mind that you won't be able to receive phone calls when you're online. You may want to put in a second line if you (or other family members, such as your teenagers) wind up spending lots of time online.

America Online has millions of faithful members because it's easy to learn, easy to use, relatively speedy, and supplies information from many different areas. As a new user, you'll appreciate its simplicity; as you work with America Online more and more, you'll come to appreciate its depth and diversity. This book introduces you to the ins and outs of AOL. You'll learn everything you need to know: how to communicate (and even procrastinate) with email, how to chat until you drop, how to surf the waves of the Web, how to do research, how to go on electronic shopping sprees, and (maybe best of all) how to get help when you get in a bind. (If you can't find what you need in this book, you can most certainly find it on AOL or on the Internet.) Dive in with a spirit of adventure!

Task

Getting Started with America Online

Welcome to America Online! Get ready to start on a great new adventure with AOL's online service. What does this new online world have to offer you? It's a great place to make new friends or gather with life-long buddies to discuss politics, new movies, or even the weather. You'll have access to an ever-expanding collection of databases with information on subjects from airplanes to zoology—plus dictionaries, encyclopedias, and news headlines 24 hours a day.

AOL also has dozens of interactive games. Whether you like role-playing, strategy, or one-on-one games, AOL's **Games** area provides you with many fun-filled hours. If you're looking for people with common interests, join one of the many online clubs. And there's more—AOL also gives you access to everything on the Internet, including the popular World Wide Web. If this new adventure sounds a little bit intimidating, don't worry. This book takes you step by step through the basics until you're ready to step out on your own. ●

How to Install America Online for Windows

After turning on your computer, the basic installation procedure for AOL is simple. If you're running Windows, you may be able to use the version of America Online that's provided (it might not be the latest and greatest edition) and install it by following the onscreen instructions. If you're using an installation CD, the procedure will be a little bit different; see the How-To Hints for details. Depending on the speed of your computer, the entire process should take just a few minutes. You can also grab the software from AOL's site (use the keyword **Upgrade**), which ensures you of getting the most recent version—but it may take a fair amount of time to download.

Begin

1 Choose America Online

Before starting the installation process, close any applications that you are currently using. Then open the **Online Services** folder on your desktop and double-click **America Online**. (If single-click mode is on, you can click just once instead.) If you can't find the **Online Services** folder, open the **Start** menu, choose **Programs**, choose **Online Services**, and then choose **America Online**.

Double-click

2 Choose the Appropriate Version

When the AOL **Welcome** screen opens, click the button for the appropriate version of America Online. For example, I need to use the United States version.

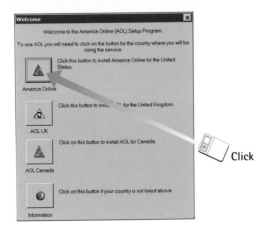

Click

3 Choose Installation Options

After a moment, the America Online installation program starts and opens a **Welcome to America Online** dialog box. In the next several windows, select the item that best describes your AOL situation and click **Next**. (If you select **Current Member** rather than **New Member**, as shown here, you'll see a slightly different set of prompts than what you see here.)

4 Choose a Directory

This screen indicates where the AOL software will be installed. The default directory is **C:\America Online 5.0**. It's best to go with the default unless you have a good reason not to. (If you want to install AOL somewhere else, click the **Expert Install** button and choose a different directory.) Then click **Next**.

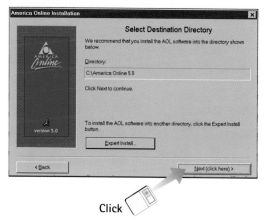

Click

5 Install AOL

AOL begins to install itself. The progress indicator in the **Installing** dialog box shows the progress of your installation; in addition, AOL displays some informational messages on the screen. (If for some reason you decide to cancel the installation, you can click the **Cancel** button. If you do this, however, you'll have to restart the installation from scratch.) The installation should go fairly quickly, and then you'll be ready to complete some easy setup steps, as described in the next task.

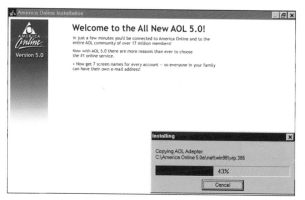

End

How-To Hints

Installing from Disk

To install AOL from disk, first insert your AOL 5 installation disk in the appropriate drive. If you're installing from a CD-ROM, the installation program should launch automatically. You should see the Welcome window shown in Step 3.

Understanding Drive Letters

If you're installing from disk, you need to know the drive letter of the disk drive you're using to install AOL for Windows. If you're using a CD-ROM, check in **My Computer** on your Windows desktop. The CD-ROM drive is represented by a CD-ROM disk icon. The icon is labeled with the drive letter—usually drive D or E.

How to Access AOL

You installed AOL onto your hard drive in the preceding task, but you still need to supply information about how you'll be connecting to AOL and which access numbers you want to use to dial in. If you're signing on with a modem, you should set up several phone numbers for dialing in to AOL. Make sure that the numbers are all in your local dialing area so that you don't incur additional long-distance charges when you sign on. Also find out the maximum speed of your modem. Each access number in AOL's listing has a reference to a modem speed (for example, 28.8Kbps or 56Kbps). Selecting phone numbers that accommodate faster modem speeds is to your advantage if you have a high-speed modem.

Begin

1 Get Connected

If you followed the steps in the preceding task, you should see this **AOL Setup** dialog box that has to do with connecting to AOL. Make sure that your modem is turned on (if you have an external modem) and connected to a phone line. Then click **Next** to proceed.

Click

2 Select a Connection

The setup software will take a few moments to check your computer for a modem or network interface card. (You'll see a message to this effect.) Then you'll be asked to select your connection. To use your modem to connect to AOL, select the **Modem** option and click **Next** (if you are using a network connection, please refer to the How-To Hints).

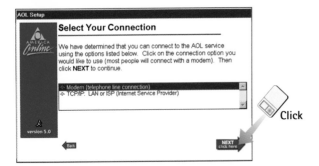

Click

3 Describe Your Phone Service

Identify the country and the area code from which you're dialing and then click **Next**. In the subsequent window, **Get AOL Access Phone Numbers Online**, you may need to specify information about your phone service, such as whether you need to dial 9 to reach an outside line. Click **Next** when you're done. The software will now automatically dial your modem to complete the setup; you may see a message that AOL is hunting for access numbers.

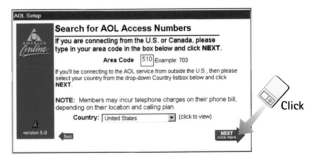

Click

4 Choose Access Numbers

When the **Select AOL Access Phone Numbers** window opens, you can begin choosing access numbers. The phone numbers on the left are AOL access numbers available in your area code. The list box on the right is for the access numbers you want to use when connecting to AOL. To add a number to your access list, select an access number from the list box on the left and click **Add**.

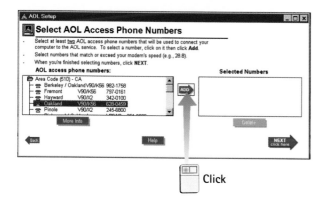

Click

5 Add and Edit Access Numbers

An **Add AOL Access Phone Number** window opens, enabling you to edit the selected number if necessary. (You can type a revised number, add the area code if needed, or click **Edit** to change dialing options—turning off call waiting, for example.) Click **Next** to finish adding the number to your access list.

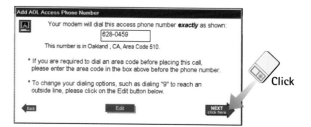

Click

6 Add More Access Numbers

Repeat Steps 4 and 5 to add more numbers to your list. You'll want to add several numbers; America Online will dial them sequentially if the first number is busy. When you have finished adding access numbers, click **Next**. Check the next task for details on how to proceed from here. (By the way, you can change access numbers after you've installed AOL by going to the **Sign On** screen and clicking the **Access Numbers** button.)

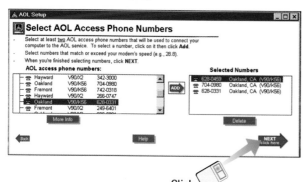

Click

End

How-To Hints

Disabling Call Waiting

You must turn off call waiting to keep from being disconnected from AOL by incoming calls. You can do so in the **Get AOL Access Phone Numbers Online** window described in Step 3. If you need to do this after your initial installation, click **Setup** in the **Sign On** screen, click **Expert Setup**, select a number, and click **Edit**. In the **Edit Number** window, select the option **Dial *70 to Disable Call Waiting** and then click **OK** to save your changes. (The *70 prefix works in many but not all areas.) The call waiting feature will be restored when you disconnect from AOL. Repeat this procedure for each access number on your list.

How to Sign On to AOL for the First Time

After you've set up your access numbers, it's time to sign on to AOL for the first time. This process is fairly automated; however, you should make some preparations ahead of time. If you installed from disk, locate the registration number and password that came with your installation disk. You must also decide how you're going to pay for your AOL membership; have that information ready. Finally, pick out several screen names for yourself. A *screen name* is a unique nickname of 3 to 16 characters (including spaces) that you use to identify yourself to AOL.

Begin

1 Connect to AOL

When you clicked **Next** in the last step of the previous task, your AOL software began dialing one of the access numbers you selected. A dialog box displays the progress of your connection. (If you installed from a disk, you may be asked to provide your registration number and password at this point. Type these numbers carefully and then click **Next**.) Then you'll be asked whether to create a new account or use an existing account. Choose the option that matches your situation (for this task, I selected the first option). Click **Next**.

Click

2 Provide Personal Information

AOL asks you to provide some personal information. Type the necessary information and click **Next**. You'll be given information on how AOL membership works. Click **Next**. You'll be asked to select a billing method; after you select a payment method, you must supply and verify your billing information. Click **Next** again. Read the **Conditions of AOL Membership** screen and click **Next** to continue.

Click

3 Choose a Screen Name

AOL asks you to choose a screen name, which serves as your identity on AOL. Type your screen name and click **Next**. If the screen name is already in use, AOL suggests an alternative name or allows you to try again. Because you can't change your master (initial) screen name, AOL asks you to confirm your screen name. To change your screen name, click the **Choose A Different Screen Name** button. Otherwise, click **Next** to continue.

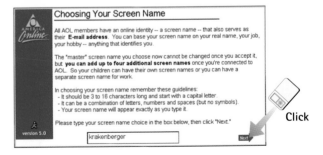
Click

4 Choose a Password

You must enter a password to keep your account secure from anyone else using it. Make sure that you type the same password in each box and click **Next**. (AOL passwords are *not* case sensitive—that is, you can enter them in uppercase or lowercase letters.) You may be asked a variety of questions, such as whether you have a CD-ROM drive, and whether you want AOL to serve as your default Internet application. Click appropriate answers.

5 Store Your Password

You'll be asked whether you want to store your password so that you don't have to type it in each time you sign on. If you decide to do this, enter your password twice and click **OK**. You'll see a message that the password has been saved for sign on. This makes it more convenient to sign on, but is not a wise idea if you share the computer with a number of people—anyone who knows your screen name will be able to access your account.

Click

6 Sign On to AOL

At long last, you'll see a **Sign On** window. Your screen name should appear in the **Select Screen Name** list box. Click the **Sign On** button (or press **Enter**) to sign on to the AOL service. You'll see a **Welcome** window (if you have a sound card, you may even hear a cheery voice welcoming you to AOL). Then the **AOL QuickStart** window appears (the QuickStart feature is discussed in Task 12, "How to Get Help in the QuickStart Area" later in this part; for now, you can close this window by choosing **No, maybe next time**).

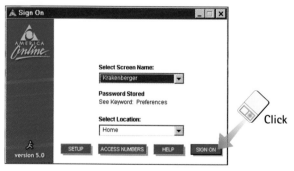

Click

End

How-To Hints

The Initial Sign On Process May Vary

Because AOL is constantly changing, what you see on your computer screen may differ from the windows shown here. You're also bound to see a few different screens if you're upgrading from a previous version of AOL rather than starting from scratch. Just read each message carefully and follow the directions on the onscreen prompts.

Choosing a Password

When choosing a password, be sure to specify one that you'll remember but that no one else is likely to guess. Of course, your password's no good if you don't remember it, so make sure that you come up with something you'll remember.

How to Leave and Return to AOL

After you've signed on to America Online, it's important to know how to sign off. Signing off from AOL disconnects your modem—hangs up your phone—so that your family can now receive regular telephone calls. AOL provides two methods of signing off: **Sign Off** and **Exit**. Both disconnect your modem, but **Exit** also automatically closes your AOL software. Each method has its advantages.

Begin

1 Sign Off

Any time you're online, you'll find a **Sign Off** menu on the menu bar. To sign off from AOL but keep the AOL for Windows software running, choose **Sign Off** from the **Sign Off** menu.

Click

2 Disconnect from AOL

Your computer disconnects from AOL, and the **Goodbye from America Online!** window opens (if you have speakers and a sound card, you may hear a happy voice wishing you "goodbye"). To exit AOL for Windows from this screen (that is, to shut down the program), choose **File, Exit** as described next. To sign back on to AOL, skip to Step 5.

3 Sign Off and Exit

If you want to sign off from AOL and exit AOL for Windows, choose **File, Exit**. AOL shuts down and any open AOL windows close; you are returned to the desktop or to another open program.

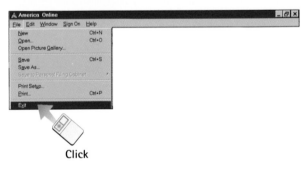

Click

4 Close and Restart AOL

To sign back on to AOL for Windows, double-click the **America Online 5.0** shortcut on your desktop (click once if single-click mode is enabled). If you're running Windows, you can click the AOL icon on the **Quick Launch** toolbar—typically, it's at the bottom of your screen on your taskbar. (Alternatively, click the **Start** button, choose **Programs**, select **America Online**, and click **America Online 5.0**.) A **Sign On** window opens.

Quick Launch toolbar

 Double-click

6 Reconnect to AOL

AOL for Windows dials one of your local access numbers, makes the connection to America Online, and checks your password. If your sign on is successful, you are welcomed back to AOL.

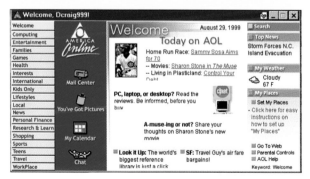

End

5 Sign Back On

Whether you see the **Goodbye from AOL!** window or the **Sign On** window, you can sign back on by typing your password in the **Enter Password** text box (for security reasons, your password displays as asterisks). Click **Sign On** if you're in the **Sign On** window; click **Sign On Again** if you're in the **Goodbye** window.

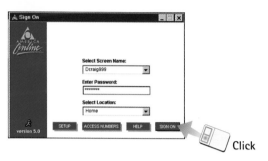

Click

How-To Hints

Reopening the Sign On Screen

When you sign off of AOL, the **Sign Off** menu changes into a **Sign On** menu. If you accidentally close the **Sign On** screen, you can retrieve it by choosing **Sign On, Sign On Screen**.

Storing Your Password

If you want to save yourself the trouble of typing your password each time you sign on, you can store your password. To do so, make sure that you are signed on, choose **Preferences** from the **My AOL** menu, choose **Passwords**, type your password in the text box, choose whether you want to save your password for sign on and/or for your Personal Filing Cabinet (PFC), and click **OK**. If you store your password, bear in mind that anyone who has access to your computer can then use your AOL account. If you're not yet comfortable using menus, check out Task 6, "How to Use AOL Menus," and Task 8, "How to Use the Toolbar Icons." Part 2, "America Online Features," describes Personal Filing Cabinets.

How to Navigate the Welcome Window

After you've signed on to AOL, you're greeted with a **Welcome** window; if you have audio, a congenial voice exclaims, "Welcome!" This window is your entry point into many of the features of AOL. Among other things, it gives you quick access to all AOL's channels, as well as to your email and chat features. The **Welcome** window also provides **AOL Today**—a wide-ranging series of topics that change daily. You'll also find a handy search feature, news headlines, and much more. The **Welcome** window is a great place to start doing just about anything in AOL.

Begin

1 Learn What's New in AOL 5.0

If this is your first time aboard, you may see an **AOL QuickStart** window like the one shown here. You'll learn how to use the QuickStart feature in Task 12, later in this part, so for now click **No, maybe next time**.

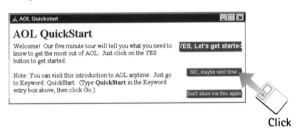

Click

2 Select a Channel

From the **Welcome** window, you can go to any of AOL's channels by clicking the channel buttons on the left side of the Welcome window (they're labeled **Welcome**, **Computing**, **Entertainment**, and so on). Channels are simply areas in which you can find information about a specific topic, such as health or travel. You'll learn more about channels in Parts 7, 8, and 9 of this book. If you need to return to the Welcome display, click the **Welcome** button.

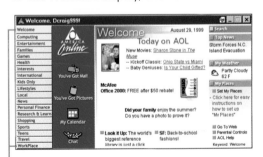

Channel buttons

3 Go to Email, Chat, and More

The **Welcome** window also gives you easy access to some of AOL's major features, such as your electronic mail (email for short) and chat rooms where you can have real-time electronic conversations. (If you have email waiting for you, a voice may say "You've got mail," and the mailbox icon will contain a letter.) You learn more about email in Part 3, "Communicating," and about chatting in Part 4, "Chatting." You can also retrieve pictures and consult your calendar from here. Check Part 2 to find out more about these exciting new features.

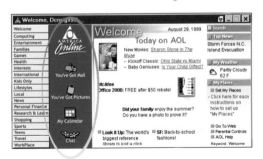

4 Check Out Today on AOL

In the center of the Welcome window is **Today on AOL**, a series of topics that change daily. Here you can find information on everything from movies to news stories to sports and more.

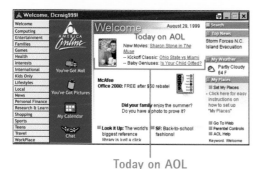

Today on AOL

5 Search for Information You Need

The **Welcome** window also lets you go to AOL's **Search** feature (click the **Search** button in the upper-right corner of the **Welcome** window, which you'll learn more about in Part 2. Using AOL **Search**, you can hunt for software (some of it free!), people, online events, books, and more.

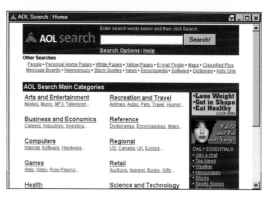

6 Check out the News and Weather

The **Welcome** window also makes it easy to read the **Top News** stories and to check out the weather. For more in-depth information on these topics, consult the **News** channel.

End

How-To Hints

Retrieving Your Welcome Window

Sometimes, your Welcome window may get shut down or buried under a pile of other open windows. It's easy enough to retrieve the Welcome window when you need it: Simply choose **Welcome** from the **Window** menu. (Actually, the option reads **Welcome** followed by your AOL screen name.) You may also have switched to a different channel by clicking one of the channel buttons described in Step 2. If so, simply click the **Welcome** button on the left side of the window.

What is "My Places"?

My Places is a new feature that lets you put topics you're interested in at your fingertips on the **Welcome** window. You learn all about setting up **My Places** in Part 2.

How to Use AOL Menus

When you start your AOL software, you'll notice the words **File**, **Edit**, **Window**, **Sign On** (or **Sign Off**), and **Help** across the top of your screen—these words make up AOL's menu bar. Each word opens a menu of items (also known as options or commands). You've probably worked with menus in other applications on your computer, and AOL's menus work in much the same way. The menus give you access to many commonly used commands. You can either click the menu name and then click an item, or you can press the **Alt** key in combination with the underlined letter in the menu name (for example, pressing **Alt+F** opens the **File** menu).

Begin

1 Open the File Menu

The **File** menu is mostly used for documents and images. You can create new documents, open existing ones, and save or print documents from this menu. And you can also exit AOL for Windows from here.

2 Open the Edit Menu

The **Edit** menu is used for editing documents. You will probably most often use this menu when editing your email (electronic mail) messages. Use the **Edit** menu options to cut, copy, and paste information in your documents. From here, you can also check your spelling and look up words in a dictionary or thesaurus. (Depending on what you're doing, many of the options in this menu may be unavailable.)

3 Open the Window Menu

The **Window** menu enables you to manipulate your windows. This menu is particularly useful if you've opened a window and cannot find it. Open windows are listed at the bottom of the menu; click the window name to bring it to the front of your screen. You can also display several open windows at a time by choosing **Cascade** or **Tile**. If you have too many windows open and want to close some of them, just click the close button (the **X**) in the upper-right corner of the window you want to close.

4 Open the Sign On Menu

Use the **Sign On** menu to display the **Sign On** screen if you've closed or misplaced it. This menu is available only if you are offline. After you've signed on to AOL, the **Sign On** menu changes to a **Sign Off** menu.

5 Open the Sign Off Menu

While you are connected to AOL, the **Sign Off** menu replaces the **Sign On** menu. The **Sign Off** menu has two options: one for signing off and one for switching screen names. You've already learned how to sign off AOL; if you want to switch to another screen name, refer to Part 6, "Sharing America Online with Your Family." When you disconnect from AOL, the **Sign Off** menu changes back to a **Sign On** menu.

6 Open the Help Menu

The **Help** menu is your centralized location for finding help with your AOL software. Online and offline help are both available; you'll learn about them in Task 10, "How to Get Offline Help" and Task 11, "How to Get Online Help," later in this part. You'll also use this menu when you need to add or change your access numbers, or when you need information about your account or the bill you receive from AOL.

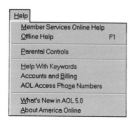

End

How-To Hints

Dialog Boxes

Menu items followed by ellipses (...) open dialog boxes that usually require you to provide additional information. For example, choosing **File, Open** displays the **File** dialog box, in which you identify the file you want to open.

Using Shortcut Keys

Many menu items have shortcut keys you can use to execute the command without going through the menu system. These shortcuts are often listed to the right of the command name in the menu. For example, you can issue the **Print** command by pressing **Ctrl+P** instead of choosing **File, Print**.

Dimmed Menu Items

Menu items are context sensitive—not all of the items are available at all times. Menu items that appear dimmed or grayed out are not currently available.

How to Use the Toolbar

The toolbar sits directly beneath the menu bar and contains icons and browser features to help you get around AOL and the Internet. You'll find out about the icons in the next task, "How to Use the Toolbar Icons." The browser features on the toolbar include a drop-down list of the last 25 places you've visited during the current session and arrows to go backward and forward between areas. You don't need to worry about getting lost on AOL. If you've forgotten how to get to that cool area you were in just a minute ago, these AOL features remember for you.

Begin

1 Explore the Toolbar

The upper part of the toolbar contains icons to take you directly to AOL areas (see the next task to learn about using these toolbar features). The lower part of the toolbar contains browsing features for use on AOL and the Internet.

Browsing features

Toolbar icons

2 Click the Arrows

Click the left (**Previous**) arrow to go back to an area you've already visited. Click the right (**Next**) arrow to return to a page after you've used the left arrow. If an arrow is dimmed, there is no page available for reloading. For example, the right arrow is dimmed if you haven't yet used the left arrow to go back to a previous area.

Next

Previous

3 Click Stop, Refresh, and Home

The **Stop** button (a circle with an **X**) enables you to stop loading the information you requested. This button is useful when you click the wrong icon or Web link (you learn more about Web links in Part 5, "Exploring the Internet") and don't want to wait for the information to finish loading. Use the **Refresh** button (the turning arrow) to refresh your screen. The **Home** button loads your Web home page or start page.

Stop | Home

Refresh

4 Click the Keyword Button

The **Keyword** button opens the **Keyword** window. Using keywords is covered in Task 9, "How to Use Keywords," later in this part.

Keyword

5 Type in the Go Text Box

Use the **Go** text box to go to a Web address or AOL area by typing the URL or keyword and clicking **Go** or pressing **Enter**. To return to one of the last 25 areas you've visited during an AOL session, click the down arrow in the **Go** text box to display the history trail and then click the location you want to return to.

Go text box

6 Click the Search Button

The **Search** button on the toolbar opens an AOL **Search** dialog box that makes it easy for you to find everything from *A* to *Z* on AOL and the Web. This dialog box also lets you go to other AOL search features—such as the White Pages and Yellow Pages—several of which you learn more about in Part 5.

Search

End

How-To Hints

Customizing the Toolbar

You can easily customize the toolbar to suit your personal preferences. To change your toolbar preferences, click the **My AOL** toolbar button and choose **Preferences**; in the **Preferences** dialog box that opens, click **Toolbar**. Options you can change include the appearance of the toolbar, its location on your screen, use of the navigation arrows, and clearing of your history trail (the list of places you've visited). From this dialog box, you can also clear your history trail anytime you're online.

Adding Favorites to the Toolbar

You can add your favorite sites to the toolbar by dragging the heart icon on the title bar of any window and dropping it on your toolbar. (You may have to delete another icon to do so; right-click that icon and choose **Remove from Toolbar**.) A **Select Icon** window appears; choose an icon and type a caption for it. The icon appears on your toolbar. (Your monitor resolution must be at least 800×600 to use this option.) You learn more about favorites in Part 2.

How to Use the Toolbar Icons

The icons on the toolbar give you quick, convenient access to many of the AOL features you will use often, such as your **Mailbox** and **Favorite Places**. Use these icons as shortcuts to areas you would otherwise access using AOL's channels or keywords (you learn about keywords in the next task). To use a toolbar icon, click it. The icon either directly accesses the area or displays a menu of features in the selected area. This task gives you a quick look at each of the icons so that you can get started. You learn more about many of these icons throughout the book.

Begin

1 Click Read, Write, and Mail Center

Click the **Read** icon to see a list of any email you've received or sent. (This icon opens the **Mailbox**, in which you can view new mail you've received, mail you've received and read already, and mail you've sent to others.) To open a form for sending email to others, click the **Write** icon. (Part 3 shows you how to send and receive email.) The **Mail Center** icon displays a menu from which you can access all of AOL's mail features.

2 Click Print

Click the **Print** icon to send the contents of the current document window to a printer. (First you'll have to fill out the **Print** dialog box to specify how many copies and a few other things.) This icon is a shortcut for choosing **File, Print**. The **Print** icon works only when the current document window contains information suitable for printing.

3 Click My Files, My AOL, and Favorites

The **My Files** icon gives you quick access to your **Personal Filing Cabinet**, **Download Manager**, and more. Click the **My AOL** icon to customize your AOL personal choices. The menu that appears when you click this icon gives you access to all the AOL preference screens and personal services such as **Buddy Lists** and **Member and News Profiles**. Click **Favorites** to open a list of your favorite places online; you find out how to build this list in Part 2.

4 Click Internet and Channels

Click the **Internet** icon to display a menu of Internet services. From here you can access the Web, FTP, newsgroups, and more. Click the **Channels** icon to directly access any AOL channel. Of course, you can also go to any of the channels by using the buttons on the left side of the **Welcome** window.

5 Click People

Click the **People** icon to display a menu of **People Connection** areas. Among other things, this menu leads to chat areas and lets you look up AOL members in the AOL Member Directory.

6 Click Quotes, Perks, and Calendar

The **Quotes** icon is a shortcut for an area in the **Personal Finances** channel. (Check Part 7 for details.) The **Perks** icon leads you to a feature that provides special deals and discounts to AOL members. The **Calendar** icon opens AOL 5.0's new calendar, which you learn how to use in Part 2.

End

How-To Hints

What's Available When You're Offline

Although six toolbar icons (**Write**, **Mail Center**, **Print**, **My Files**, **My AOL**, and **Favorites**) can be used offline, the rest are available only for online use. When toolbar icons are unavailable, they usually appear dimmed or grayed out. Some features in these areas may also not be available while you are offline.

Helpful Reminders

If you can't remember what feature or service a toolbar icon represents, point your mouse to it; a description of the service appears on your screen in a pop-out text box.

The AOL Icon

The AOL icon at the far right end of the toolbar pulsates to let you know when pages are loading, but clicking this icon doesn't do anything.

How to Use Keywords

As you become familiar with AOL and discover certain features and areas you want to visit regularly, you'll come to appreciate *keywords*. Using a keyword is like taking a taxi: You give the driver an address, and then sit back for the ride. You don't have to know the route because the driver takes care of that for you. New in town and don't know any addresses? No problem—just like a friendly and knowledgeable taxi driver, AOL provides some address suggestions for you.

Begin

1 Click the Keyword Button

To use a keyword, make sure that you're signed on to AOL. Click the **Keyword** button on the toolbar (or press **Ctrl+K**). The **Keyword** dialog box opens.

Click

2 Enter a Keyword

If you know which keyword you want to use, skip to Step 6. Otherwise, click the **Keyword List** button to display a list of keywords. (You can also type **KEYWORD** in the text box to find this list of AOL keywords.) The **Keyword** dialog box opens.

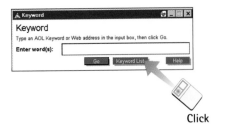

Click

3 Double-Click in the Keyword List

Keywords may be listed alphabetically, as shown here, or by channel (click the **List by Channel** tab). Double-click one of the categories to see a list of its keywords.

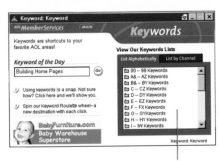

Double-click a category

4 Find a Keyword

Scroll through the list to find the area you want to visit. Note that the keyword is the word on the left end of each line. (Hold on to good keywords when you find them; not every area displays a keyword, even if there is one.) Make a mental note of the keyword you want to use, or write it down if you think that will help. Then close both **Keywords** windows by clicking their close buttons (the **X** in the upper-right corner of the window).

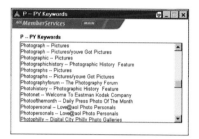

5 Type a Keyword

Back in the original **Keyword** dialog box, type your keyword in the **Enter word(s)** text box and click **Go** or press **Enter**. Note that keywords are *not* case sensitive; that is, it doesn't matter whether you type a keyword in all uppercase (**LIBRARY**), all lowercase (**library**), or some mixture of the two (**LiBrArY**). You'll still land in the same place.

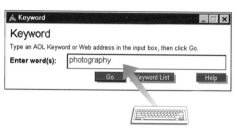

6 Go to a Keyword Area

The **Keyword** dialog box closes and you go directly to the department or area specified by your keyword (note that the keyword appears in the bottom-right corner of the window; this is where keywords are found on many pages).

End

How-To Hints

A Quick Way to Enter Keywords

If you know which keyword you want to use, you can type it in the **Go** text box at the top of the screen and click **Go** or press **Enter**.

Keywords and Favorite Places

If you use certain areas frequently, or if you have trouble remembering your favorite keywords, try adding them to **Favorite Places**. For more information on using **Favorite Places**, see Task 14, "How to Keep Track of Your Favorites," in Part 2.

Navigating with Keywords

If you use keywords to jump from one place to the next and then want to return to your original window, close or minimize any new windows you've opened. Alternatively, try returning to a previous window by choosing its name from the history trail in the toolbar (see Task 7, "How to Use the Toolbar" earlier in this part) or from the **Window** menu.

How to Get Offline Help

Why won't my new modem dial when I click **Sign On**? How can I connect to AOL when I'm away from home? How can I change my local access numbers? The answers to these and many more questions are waiting for you in Offline Help. Because some of this information may occasionally be out of date, it's best to use Offline Help only when you can't get online. For the most current information, double-check with Online Help, if possible (see the next task).

Begin

1 Getting into Offline Help

AOL for Windows should be running, but there's no need to sign on to AOL. (If you were signed on, you'd be more likely to use online help.) Then choose **Help, Offline Help** from the menu bar. (You can carry out this exercise even if you're signed on.)

2 Find a Help Topic

The **Help Topics** window opens, listing available help topics. (Your window may look somewhat different from this one.) On the **Contents** tab, notice that every help topic has a book icon.

3 Find More Help Topics

Double-click a topic. The topic listing expands to show related subjects. Notice that the icon next to the topic you selected is now an open book icon. (The long way around is to select a topic and click **Open**.)

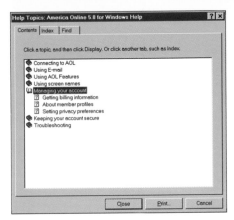

4 Display a Help Screen

Some topics have a question-mark icon to their left. These icons lead to help screens containing information about the listed subject. Double-click a subject that interests you. (You can also select the subject and click **Display**.)

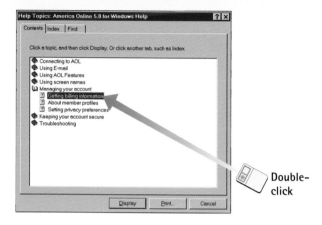

Double-click

5 Display a Definition

A window describing your subject appears. Sometimes you'll come across a word or phrase with dotted underlining; click the underlined word to display a definition of that word or phrase.

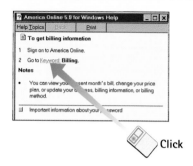

Click

6 Read and Close a Definition

After you've read the definition, click anywhere to close it. To return to the **Help Topics** window shown in Step 2, click **Help Topics** at the top of the help screen window.

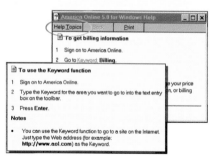

End

How-To Hints

Using the Index and Find Tabs

You can also use the **Index** tab in the **Help Topics** dialog box to hunt for help topics by name. Another convenient way to get offline help is to search for help, much as you search a searchable database (see Task 12, "How to Search a Searchable Database," in Part 2). To start searching for help, choose the **Find** tab in the **Help Topics** dialog box.

Other Ways of Getting Help

If you can't find the help you need in Offline Help, and you aren't able to sign on to AOL, there are several toll-free numbers you can call to get help: For screen name or password problems, call 888-265-8004; for access numbers, call 888-265-8005; for Windows-related issues, call 888-265-8006; for Macintosh questions, call 888-265-8007; for billing information, call 888-265-8003; and for cancellations, call 888-265-8008.

How to Get Online Help

Like Offline Help, AOL's Online Help provides screen after screen of useful solutions. Online Help takes help one step further. If you have a problem or question for which AOL has no ready answer, you still have three additional online methods for finding a solution: You can chat live in the AOL **Members Helping Members** area of the **Tech Live Auditorium**, you can post your question to AOL members through a **Members Helping Members** message board, or you can call AOL's toll-free customer support numbers. With all the prepared solutions and these three live resources, you should be able to solve just about any AOL problem.

Begin

1 Start Online Help

Make sure that you're signed on to AOL. Then choose **Help, Member Services Online Help**. The **AOL Member Services** window opens.

Click

2 View Member Services Window

Click a help topic on the left side of the window. (If you're not sure which topic to use, click **Search Help** and skip to Step 5.) The help topic window opens.

Click

3 Use the Help Topic Window

Click a subject on the left side of the window to change the listing in the text box on the right. Then double-click an item in the list box on the right to view a document about your subject.

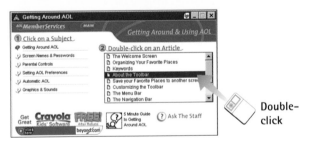

Double-click

4 Read the Help Document

Use the scrollbars as necessary to read the help document. To return to the **AOL Members Services** window, click **Main** at the top of the help document window. Alternatively, click **Search Help** and proceed to Step 5.

Click

5 Search for Help Topics

The **Search** window lets you search through the help topics for an answer to your question without having to browse through list boxes of topics. Enter a word or phrase in the text box and click **Search**.

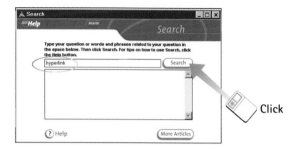

Click

6 Display the Help Document

A list of subjects relating to your search text appears in the lower text box. Double-click any item to display a help document for that subject. (The **More Articles** button becomes available if you turn up more articles than fit in the list box at one time.)

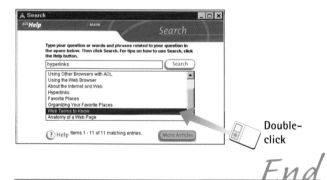

Double-click

End

How-To Hints

Finding Toll-Free Help Numbers

To find a list of the current toll-free numbers for customer assistance, click **Ask the Staff** in a topic or document window and then click **Receive Live One-on-One Help** in the **Ask the Staff** window.

Getting Help from Members

Type the keyword **MHM** to access the **Members Helping Members** area which has answers to top AOL questions and message boards where AOL members share information and experiences on AOL-related issues.

Use Help as a Resource

Don't wait until you have a problem to explore online help; it's good to know how to get help before you're baffled or in a dire situation. Besides, in addition to solutions to specific problems, online help suggests methods for using AOL more fully and efficiently.

How to Get Help in the QuickStart Area

It's invaluable to know how to use both the online and offline help systems described in the preceding tasks. But if you're new to AOL and want a little more hand holding, consider exploring the resources available in the QuickStart guide. With QuickStart, you can find tutorials, a five-minute guide to AOL, and a series of handy insider tips.

Begin

1 Open the Keyword Dialog Box

Make sure that you're signed on to AOL, and click the **Keyword** button in the toolbar or press **Ctrl+K**. The **Keyword** dialog box opens.

Click

2 Enter a Keyword

In the **Keyword** dialog box, type **quickstart** and click **Go** or press **Enter**. The **QuickStart** window opens.

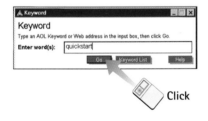

Click

3 Choose Five Minutes to AOL

In the **QuickStart** window, click **5 Minute Guide to AOL**. The QuickStart feature opens.

Click

4 Read the Introduction

The **Introduction** window gives you an overview of the five-minute tour. Click the **Forward** arrow (the right-pointing triangle) to set out on your tour.

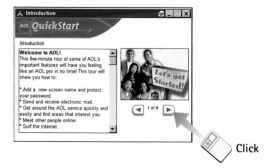

Click

5 Read About Screen Names

The second window describes what screen names and passwords are and how they work. Click the **Forward** arrow to move on to the next screen until you've read all the available screens of information. If you decide to go back at any point, simply click the **Back** arrow (the left-pointing triangle). Click the **Forward** arrow a final time in the last screen.

Click

6 Jump to Other QuickStart Areas

You'll land on this **Congratulations!** screen, which provides links that let you easily jump to other QuickStart areas such as **AOL Fast Facts** and **Meg's Insider Tips**. If you have the time or inclination, keep exploring by clicking these links. Otherwise, close the window by clicking the close button (the **X**) in the upper-right corner.

Click

End

How-To Hints

AOL FastFacts

From the initial **QuickStart** window shown in Step 3, go to the **AOL FastFacts** area to find out more about AOL's favorite features, including buddy lists, junk mail controls, and instant messages.

Match Your Interests

The **Interest Profiles** area shown in Step 3 lets you specify what areas are of interest to you—anything from politics to movies to games to computing to travel to health. After you fill out a form indicating your interests, AOL will email you about sites that jibe with your interests. See Part 2 for details on how to set up an interest profile.

AOL Tips

AOL Tips are just that: tips about a whole range of features, from email and chat rooms to the Internet. Click **AOL Tips** from the initial **QuickStart** window shown in Step 3. Then pick a general topic you want to learn more about, and from there pick a particular article you want to read.

Task

2

America Online Features

*T*he tasks in this part of the book discuss a wide array of features, most of which are exclusive to AOL. You'll discover how to use the **My AOL** feature to customize AOL to better meet your needs. You'll also find out how to sift through the enormous volumes of information available online: AOL 5.0's exciting new search feature lets you search the wide world of the Internet in addition to AOL. You'll learn where to find and download useful software applications (many of them free), and how to upload and share files you've created.

You'll also learn how to set up and schedule **Automatic AOL**—this feature enables you to compose email and choose files for downloading while you're offline and then carry out all your online activities in one fell swoop. This strategy is invaluable for keeping your phone line free if you have only a single line. In addition, you'll learn how to maintain your **Personal Filing Cabinet**, an area in which each AOL user can store sent and received email, a list of downloaded files, and a list of sent or received newsgroup postings. You'll also find out how to set up a news profile that tells AOL which types of news articles you want to receive directly in your mailbox. New to AOL 5.0 is the *interest profile*; you indicate your areas of interest, and AOL sends you periodic emails describing AOL sites you might find relevant.

You also learn some strategies for finding other AOL members. You discover how to record your **Favorite Places** so that you can easily go back to AOL sites and Internet sites you've already visited and want to see again. The **Calendar** is another cool new AOL 5.0 feature that lets you keep track of your own appointments and also hunt down events and festivities in your area.

Finally, your distant relatives should be thrilled about "You've Got Pictures." This new feature lets you take your film to a participating photo developer and pick up your photos...*on AOL!* ●

How to Use My AOL

While exploring AOL, you may already have noticed preferences windows that allow you to customize your session's sounds, fonts, and more. The **My AOL** area lets you set the preferences for any or all your activities in one stop. **My AOL** also includes many personal services. For instance, you can set up a stock portfolio or create a personal Web page or a news profile. **My AOL** has too many features to show here, so this task just gets you started. You'll have opportunities to explore other **My AOL** areas throughout this book.

Begin

1 Access My AOL

Make sure that you're signed on to AOL. Then click the **My AOL** icon on the toolbar and choose **My AOL** from the menu that appears. The **My AOL** window opens.

Click

2 Choose Preferences Guide

Take a look around the **My AOL** window to see what is available here. Click the **Preferences** link to continue. The **Preferences** window opens.

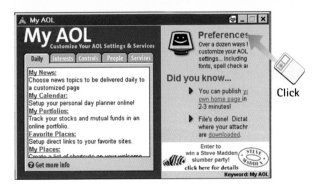

Click

3 View the Preferences Window

The **Preferences** window contains three columns listing different categories—**Account Controls**, **Communications**, and **Organization**—for which you can set up preferences. Read the description for the **Personal Filing Cabinet** option under **Organization**. (You learn how to use your Personal Filing Cabinet in Task 9, later in this part.)

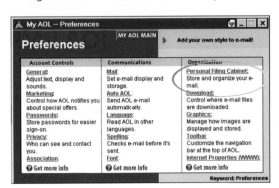

4 Choose Which Preferences to Set

Click the **Personal Filing Cabinet** option to select it. A **Personal Filing Cabinet Preferences** window opens. (If you prefer, you can choose any other preferences area that interests you.) If you send and receive lots of email, your Personal Filing Cabinet file can grow very large very quickly.

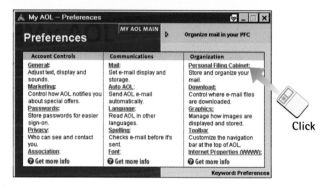

Click

5 Personal Filing Cabinet Preferences

The **Personal Filing Cabinet Preferences** window lets you specify when you want to be warned about the size of the PFC file. If hard disk space is at a premium, enter a lower value than the default of 10 megabytes. (You should increase the value only if you are receiving error messages and have plenty of hard disk space for storing additional email.) You can also change the default value for the "free space" option, which warns you about fragmentation of your PFC file. You can also choose whether to be asked for confirmation when deleting files from your Personal Filing Cabinet. Unless you never make mistakes, it's best to leave these options selected. When you have finished making changes, click **OK**.

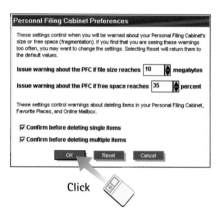

Click

6 Set Additional Preferences

Back in the main **Preferences** window, you can click another preferences option to set up additional preferences if you want. When you finish setting preferences, close the **Preferences** window by clicking the close button in the upper-right corner or return to the main **My AOL** window by clicking the **My AOL Main** button (look for it at the top of the window).

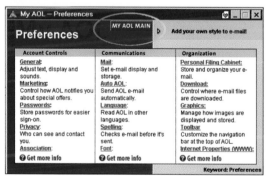

End

How-To Hints

A Shortcut

An alternative way to change your preferences is to choose **Preferences** from the **My AOL** menu. This option leads to a **Preferences** window, from which you can choose categories such as **General**, **Toolbar**, **Mail**, and so on. The disadvantage of this **Preferences** window is that it doesn't provide the handy and helpful descriptions you saw in this task.

How to Use AOL Search

AOL 5.0 has a new search feature that lets you search both AOL and the Web with equal ease. In this task, you learn the ins and outs of how to use this feature. But this is just the beginning of searching for information you need on AOL and the Web. In the next task, you learn how to search for files to download. In addition, in Part 5, "Exploring the Internet," you'll find out how to use some special search features to find both people and businesses on the Internet. Searching for—and finding—the online resources you need is what using AOL is all about.

Begin

1 Choose the Search Button

Make sure that you're signed on to AOL. Then click the **Search** button in the upper-right corner of the screen. The **AOL Search** window opens. In the text box at the top of the screen, you can type words or phrases to find. Alternatively, you can choose from a series of categories, such as **Science and Technology**, **Business and Economics**, and **Reference**.

2 Type in a Search Word or Phrase

Type a search word or phrase in the text box and click **Search** or press **Enter**.

3 Browse the Search Results Window

If the search is successful, you'll see an **AOL Search Results** window something like the one shown here. Notice that this window tells you how many categories match your search criteria. (In this example, the search string **evolution** may be found in 238 categories such as **Science > Biology > Evolution** and so on.) The window also shows how many sites matched your search criteria (in this case, well over 4,000!)

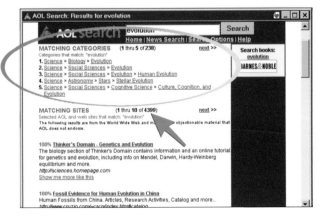

4 Select a Topic

If you find something of interest, click the link to open a window containing the article on that topic. Scroll to read the article. (You may be able to follow links to more sites of interest.) When you're done, click the **Previous** button in the toolbar until you return to the **AOL Search** window.

Click

6 Narrow the Search Further

Just searching AOL, rather than the default of AOL and the Web, is one way of narrowing your search. You can narrow your search further by using multiple search criteria. For example, if you search for **evolution** and **Kansas** (just separate the two words with a space in the **Search** text box), you'll turn up many fewer matches—a Very Good Thing given the overwhelming magnitude of information on AOL and on the Web.

5 Choosing Where to Search

Back in the **AOL Search** window, click **Search Options** (under the **Search** text box) to see how to make your search more specific. In the resulting **Search Options** window, you can choose to search only AOL, only the Web, or both (the default). When you've made your selections, click the **Search** button as usual. Scroll through the results to see whether you unearthed something that seems suitable. If so, click the link to read up on it.

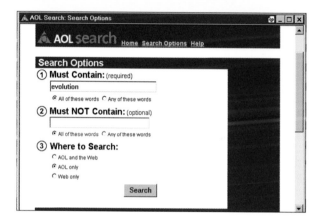

How-To Hints

Refining Your Search

There are additional ways to narrow your search. As you learned, if you search for multiple words (separated by spaces), you'll find only information relevant to *both* topics (both **evolution** and **Kansas**, for instance). You can also search for exact phrases by enclosing them within quotation marks. What's more, you can *exclude* topics from your search by preceding them with the word **not**; for example, "**Evolution not Kansas**" finds everything having to do with evolution that doesn't have to do with the decision in Kansas. (If you're in the **Search Options** window, you can do this by including words in the **Must NOT Contain** text box.)

End

How to Search for a Downloadable File

AOL's search feature is extremely handy for finding *downloadable files*—that is, files you can transfer to your computer and then use. AOL's downloadable files are organized into specialized file collections called *software libraries*. Software libraries, which are found in many AOL areas, are usually indicated by buttons or list box items that display a stack of floppy disks. (Software libraries can include not only software but also images, sounds, and more.) These libraries are sometimes limited in scope and can occasionally be difficult to find. Rather than trying to work with these individual libraries, you can get central access to most downloadable files by using one of AOL's searchable databases of files.

Begin

1 Choose the Keyword Button

Make sure that you're signed on to AOL and click the **Keyword** button on the toolbar. The **Keyword** window opens.

Click

2 Enter Find Software

Enter the keyword **find software** in the **Enter word(s)** text box. Then click **Go** or press **Enter**. The **Find Software** window opens.

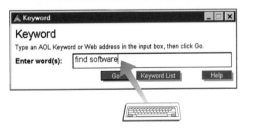

3 Search for Shareware

From this window, you can search either for shareware or for brand-name software. For this task, click **Search for Shareware**. The **PC Download Center** window opens.

 Click

4 Choose a Category of Software

Make sure that the **Shareware** tab is selected under **Download Catalogue**. (If you want to hunt for brand-name software, click the **Buy Software** tab instead—but be aware that the search process is fairly different.) Then double-click one of the software categories in the list box to bring up a window full of software libraries in that category. For example, if you double-click **Internet Tools,** you'll see a window listing various categories of Internet software and their associated libraries.

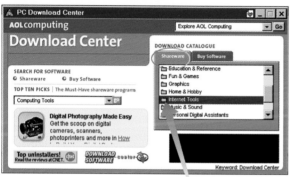

Double-click

5 Select a Category and a Software Library

From this window, double-click a category in the left list box (if the desired category is not selected already) and double-click a software library that interests you in the right list box. You'll see a window listing the files available for downloading in that software library.

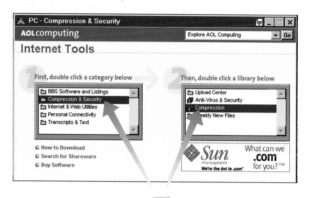

Double-click

6 Read the File Description

Look for a file that interests you. (Scroll if necessary, or click the **List More Files** button to display additional files in the list box.) Click the filename and then click **Read Description** to open a detailed description of the selected file. Read this description carefully—paying close attention to the estimated time it will take to download the file and the computer equipment and software necessary.

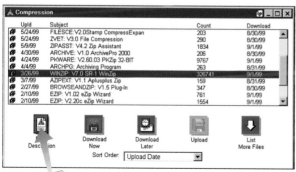

Click

How-To Hints

Downloading Files

For information about downloading files after you've found them, see the next task.

Narrowing Your Search

You can use the **Search for Shareware** button (available in the window shown in Step 5) to open the **Software Search** dialog box. From there, you can narrow your search by limiting the search to certain categories of software. In addition, you can choose the **Past Month** or **Past Week** radio button to search for only the more-recent files. You can narrow the search further by typing one or more search criteria at the bottom of the window. When you're ready to go, click **Search**.

End

How to Download a File

After you've found a file that meets your needs, you might want to download it. You should exercise caution when downloading files: Files on the Internet may contain *viruses* that can cause serious damage to your system. Make sure that any files you download are from a *trusted source*. Software you download from an AOL software library should have been carefully screened. But take great care when downloading files from the Net or when handling attached files you've received from someone you don't know. (You'll learn more about sending and receiving files attached to email in Part 3 "Communicating.") If you download lots of stuff but you also want to protect yourself, consider purchasing (or downloading!) some antivirus software.

Begin

1 Initiate the Download

Use the steps described in Task 3 to locate and read about the file you want to download. After you decide for sure to download a file, click **Download Now**. (You can click this button whether you're reading the file's description or just viewing the list of downloadable files.) The **Download Manager** window opens.

Click

2 Choose a Location

Use the **Download Manager** window to specify where on your computer to place the file you're downloading. Files are placed in the **Download** directory by default. To specify a new location for the file, pull down the **Save In** drop-down list and choose a directory in which to save the file.

Click

3 Enter a Filename

You can also rename the file being downloaded by typing a new name in the **File name** text box. (The existing filename is selected automatically, so you can just start typing to overwrite it with the new filename.)

4 Complete the Download

To proceed with the download, click **Save** in the **Download Manager** window. A **File Transfer** dialog box opens, displaying the progress of your file transfer. (Remember that *download* and *file transfer* mean the same thing: moving files from another location *down* to your computer so that you can use them.)

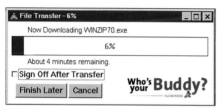

5 Confirm the Download

When the download is complete, you'll see a dialog box to that effect. If you have working audio, you may hear a computerized voice telling you "file's done." Click **OK** to close the dialog box.

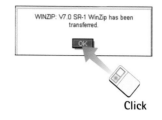

Click

End

How-To Hints

Finding Downloaded Files

After you've downloaded a file, by default it's on your hard disk in the *directory* (a subsection of the disk) specified by the **Download Manager** window shown in Step 2. By default, this directory is **c:\America Online 5.0\download**. But if you changed the directory in Step 2, the file is in the directory you specified.

Working with Compressed Files

If you download a file that has an extension such as **.ZIP**, **.ARJ**, **.Z**, or **.TAR**, the file has been stored in a compressed format to save download time. (These are often known as "zipped" files.) After the file is downloaded, you'll need to uncompress it to use it. For details on how to do this, check the documentation for your unzipping program.

Help with Downloading

If you're feeling a bit overwhelmed about the whole downloading process, you may want to get help. In the **PC Download Center** window (see Step 4 in Task 3), double-click **How to Download** under **Shareware** to open a whole screen full of options for educating yourself about downloading.

Stopping the File Transfer

It's supremely easy to stop a file transfer that's underway. If you decide against it altogether, click the **Cancel** button in the **File Transfer** window. If you decide not to carry out the transfer right at this moment (maybe it's going to take forever, and you don't have that long), click **Finish Later** and pick up where you left off at another time. (To do this, track down the file to download, click the **Download Now** button again, and respond **Yes** when asked if you want to continue the download.)

How to Use the Download Manager

In the previous task, you learned how to download a single file. But what if you want to download more than one file at a time, or what if you don't want to start downloading files until after you've finished something more pressing? (Even if you have a pretty speedy modem, some downloads can take a *long* time.) In any case, you can use AOL's **Download Manager**. The **Download Manager** is essentially a to-do list, keeping track of every file you decide to download. As you perform multiple file searches or explore multiple software libraries, you add files to the list. Then when you're ready to download, you tell the **Download Manager** to download every selected file, all at once.

Begin

1 Choose Download Later

After you've searched for and found a file you want to download, select it and click **Download Later** rather than **Download Now** (you can do this either in the description window or in the window showing the file search results).

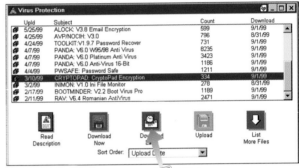

Click

2 Close the Confirmation Dialog Box

A dialog box informs you that the selected file has been added to your download list. Click **OK** to close this dialog box.

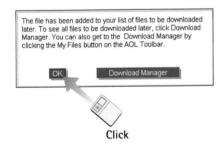

Click

3 Choose More Files to Download

Repeat Steps 1 and 2 for each file you want to download; feel free to explore AOL between adding files to your list. When you're ready to start the download, click the **My Files** icon on the toolbar and select **Download Manager**. (If you're ready to download immediately after adding the last file to your list, you can click **Download Manager** rather than **OK** in the confirmation dialog box shown in Step 2.)

Click

4 Initiate the Download

If you're asked for your password, enter it in the dialog box that appears. A **Download Manager** window opens, listing the files you've chosen to download. Click **Download**.

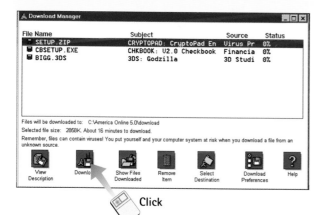

Click

5 Track the Download's Progress

A **File Transfer** dialog box shows the progress of each file as it downloads and indicates how much longer the download will take. For lengthy downloads, check the **Sign Off After Transfer** box and then turn your attention to other matters. AOL for Windows then automatically downloads your files, signing off when it's done.

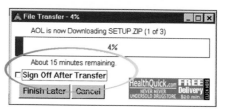

6 View the Download Status

When the download is complete, you'll hear the message "file's done," and the **File Transfer Status** window will indicate that the files were transferred. Click **Show Files Downloaded** in the **Download Manager** window to confirm that your files were indeed downloaded. (You'll see a list of all the files you've downloaded—not just the files from this session.)

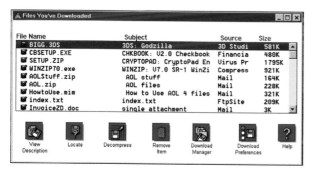

End

How-To Hints

Using the Download Manager While Signed Off

Even after you've signed off from AOL, the **Download Manager** can still serve several purposes. Click the **My Files** toolbar button and choose **Download Manager** to see a list of files you've selected for downloading but haven't yet downloaded. Click **Show Files Downloaded** to open a list showing the files you've downloaded to this point, as mentioned in Step 6.

More Download Manager Features

From within the **Download Manager**, you can carry out a number of other downloading chores: If you decide against downloading one or more particular files, you can select them and click the **Remove Item** button. You can choose **Select Destination** to choose where to place the downloaded files (they're stashed in your AOL **Download** directory by default). You can also choose **Download Preferences** to set your preferences about how you want downloads to occur.

How to Upload a File

Have you created a great game, a cool program, a screen saver, or just some helpful tips? Why not share your favorite programs, graphics, and computer expertise with other AOL members? Uploading is easy, and it's one more way for you to contribute to the collective information on AOL. Just make sure that the file you're uploading is freeware, shareware, or your own creation, and be certain to send a complete set of files. (If you're sending in multiple files, you'll typically want to zip them into a single file before you begin your upload.)

Begin

1 Enter the Keyword Upload

Make sure that you're signed on to AOL, and then click the **Keyword** button on the toolbar. In the **Keyword** window, type **upload** and click **Go**. The **PC Upload Center** window opens.

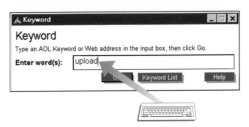

2 Choose Where to Upload

Select the appropriate forum for your upload and click **Open**. The forum's **Uploading** window opens.

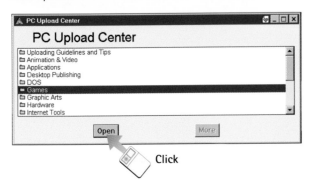

Click

3 Initiate the Upload

If you're not familiar with uploading in general, or have never uploaded to a particular forum, read the guidelines for that forum before you initiate your download. (They'll most likely be called **Guidelines for Uploading Files** or something similar. In the screen shown here, you would choose **FILES: BEFORE YOU UPLOAD.**) From this window, click **Upload**. The forum's **Uploading** dialog box opens.

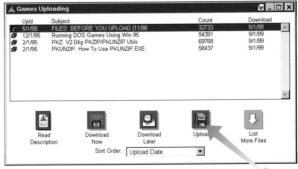

Click

4 Enter Upload Information

Enter the information regarding your upload in the dialog box; be sure to include a brief description of the file or files you're uploading. (The information shown here is just an example; there's no need for you to type it in.) Then click **Select File** to open the **Attach File** dialog box.

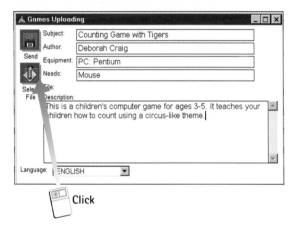

Click

5 Choose the File to Upload

Select the location and name of the file you're uploading, and then click **Open**. (If you need help finding your file, consult your Windows documentation.) You return to the **Uploading** dialog box. Notice that the name of the file you selected now appears to the right of the word **File** in the middle of the dialog box. (You can choose only a single file here, so if you want to upload a set of files, you'll most likely need to zip them into a single file first. Check your forum's uploading guidelines for details.)

Click

6 Start the Upload

Click **Send** in the **Uploading** dialog box to begin the upload. A **File Transfer** dialog box opens to display the progress of the file transfer from your computer to AOL. The length of this transfer depends primarily on the file's size and the speed of your modem. After the file transfer is complete, another dialog box informs you of that fact. Click the **OK** button to close this dialog box.

Click

End

How-To Hints

Finding a Compression Program

As mentioned, to upload multiple files that go with a single program you may need to compress them into one file. The added benefit of this approach is that the file will upload more quickly and will be easier for other users to download. If you need a compression program, click AOL's **Search** button, choose the option **Software**, click **Search for Shareware**, choose **Utilities & Tools**, choose the **File Utilities** category, and investigate the various compression options. Again, you may want to check the uploading guidelines for various forums for recommended compression programs. PKZIP and WinZip are two very popular and widely available alternatives.

How to Set Up Automatic AOL

Automatic AOL can serve as your electronic personal assistant. You tell AOL what types of activities you need it to do (send and receive mail, send and receive newsgroup postings, or download files), and it does them—day or night, on a schedule or on demand—as often as you want. You just leave the AOL software running but don't sign on. When Automatic AOL runs, it signs on for you, does what it needs to do, and then signs off again.

Begin

1 Choose Set Up Automatic AOL

Start AOL for Windows (you don't have to sign on, although it's fine if you're already signed on). Click the **Mail Center** toolbar icon and choose **Set Up Automatic AOL**. The **Welcome to Automatic AOL** window opens. (If instead you see the **Automatic AOL** window, click the **Walk Me Through** button.)

Click

2 Begin Setting Up Automatic AOL

Click **Continue** to choose a walk-through that guides you through the process of setting up Automatic AOL. In the next several windows, you specify which activities you want to occur during your Automatic AOL session. (If you feel fairly sure-footed, you can instead click **Expert Setup** to set up Automatic AOL just by selecting or deselecting various check boxes—without any special guidance.)

Click

3 Retrieve Unread Mail

Click **Yes** in the **Retrieve Unread Mail** window if you want Automatic AOL to download new mail you have not read online so that you can read your mail offline. (Downloaded mail is placed in your Personal Filing Cabinet, and downloaded files are placed in the directory specified in the **Download Manager**.) This option takes you to the **Download Files** window. Clicking **Yes** here causes AOL to automatically download any files attached to your incoming mail. If you select **No**, you can log on and download these files later.

Click

4 Send Outgoing Mail

Click **Yes** in the **Send Outgoing Mail** window if you want to automatically send any mail you've prepared and marked to **Send Later** (see the How-To Hints at the end of this task).

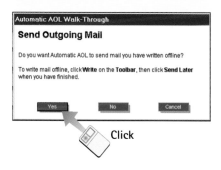

Click

5 Download Files

Click **Yes** in the **Download Files in the Download Manager** window if you want to download any files saved in the **Download Manager**. (You learned how to use the **Download Manager** in Task 5, earlier in this part.)

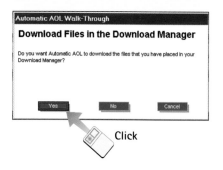

Click

6 Retrieve and Send Postings

If you want to retrieve unread postings in newsgroups you're subscribed to, click **Yes** in the **Retrieve Unread Postings** window. (You learn about newsgroups in Part 5.) Click **Yes** in the **Send Outgoing Postings** window if you want to automatically send postings to your newsgroups. At this point, you are ready to schedule Automatic AOL, as described in the next task. The easiest approach is to jump straight to the next task now. However, if you choose which screen names to affect and press **Continue**, you can also schedule Automatic AOL at a later time by choosing **Run Automatic AOL** from the **Mail Center** menu.

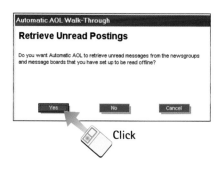

Click

End

How-To Hints

Sending Email Later

To send mail in AOL during an Automatic AOL session rather than right away, use the **Send Later** button in the **Write Mail** window. (See Part 3 for more information on composing mail.)

Composing Messages Offline

You can compose all your email messages and Internet newsgroup messages offline and then activate an Automatic AOL session to sign on and send them. This is a particularly useful strategy if you're paying for connect charges or if you don't want to tie up your phone line.

Personal Filing Cabinets

Each screen name has its own Personal Filing Cabinet with an incoming mailbox, outgoing mailbox, and Download Manager. (Turn to Task 9, "How to Use Your Personal Filing Cabinet," for more information on using your Personal Filing Cabinet.)

How to Schedule Automatic AOL

After you set up your Automatic AOL activities as described in Task 7, you'll need to tell AOL which of the screen names you want to run the activities for and schedule when and how often you want to connect to AOL automatically. AOL has two options for running Automatic AOL: right now (anytime you tell it to) or on a schedule you determine. Whether it runs during the night while you're sleeping or during the day while you're at work, Automatic AOL's Scheduler ensures that your mail and Internet newsgroups will be taken care of while you're busy with other matters. Also, your phone line no longer has to be monopolized by downloading when important calls may be coming in.

Begin

1 Select Screen Names

From the dialog box that appears after you complete Step 6 in the preceding task, select the screen name or names to use during your Automatic AOL sessions. Enter the appropriate password next to each screen name. (See Part 6, "Sharing America Online with Your Family," for more information about using multiple screen names in a single account.) Then click **Continue**. The **Schedule Automatic AOL** window opens.

Click

2 Schedule Automatic AOL to Run

If you want to schedule Automatic AOL to run at specific times on specific days, click **Yes**. The **Which Days of the Week** window opens. (If you want to run Automatic AOL manually, click **No** and see the How-To Hint titled "Running Automatic AOL Now.")

Click

3 Choose Which Days Will Run

Use the check boxes to select the day(s) on which you want your Automatic AOL sessions to occur. When you are ready, click **Continue**. The **How Often Each Day** window opens.

Click

4 Set the Frequency

Click the appropriate option button in the **How Often Each Day** window to set the frequency for your Automatic AOL sessions and then click **Continue**. The **Starting Time Each Day** window opens.

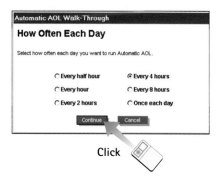

Click

5 Set the Starting Time

Specify the time at which you want your first Automatic AOL session to occur. Use the up and down arrows to set the time in hours and minutes. Time is set based on the 24-hour clock, so if you want an Automatic AOL session to occur at 11:00 p.m., set the starting time to **23:00**. Because the Scheduler relies on your computer's internal clock, make sure that it is set correctly. (If you're not sure how to do this, check your Windows documentation for more information.) When you're ready, click **Continue**.

Click

6 Exit the Walk-Through

Congratulations, you've now set up your Automatic AOL session(s). Make sure that you leave your computer on with the AOL for Windows software running. (AOL can't run all these tasks automatically if your computer's not up and running!) Click **OK** to exit the walk-through.

Click

End

How-To Hints

Staying Safe

When you set up Automatic AOL, you store your password so that unattended sessions can take place. Make sure that only those whom you trust will have access to your computer.

Running Automatic AOL Now

To run Automatic AOL right now (as opposed to at some scheduled time in the future), click the **Mail Center** icon on the toolbar and choose **Run Automatic AOL**. In the **Run Automatic AOL Now** window, click **Begin** to start Automatic AOL. AOL dials your modem, logs you in to AOL, and carries out the tasks you specified when you set up Automatic AOL.

How to Use Your Personal Filing Cabinet

All screen names listed under your account have their own Personal Filing Cabinet to help keep track of Automatic AOL downloads, incoming and outgoing mail, and incoming and outgoing Internet newsgroup messages. Each screen name's user can personalize his or her Personal Filing Cabinet by using the mouse to drag and drop the files and folders in the user's own area. In addition, if you're worried about your spouse or child accidentally reading your mail and finding out about that surprise you've been planning for months, you can add a password that is requested when anyone tries to open your Personal Filing Cabinet.

Begin

1 Open the Personal Filing Cabinet

Click the **My Files** icon on the toolbar and choose **Personal Filing Cabinet**. (If you have sub-accounts, you must first select your screen name in the **Select Screen Name** box in the **Sign On** or **Goodbye from America Online!** window.) Your **Filing Cabinet** window opens.

Click

2 Explore the Mail Folder

The Personal Filing Cabinet is divided into folder areas for **Mail**, **Newsgroups**, and **Download Manager**. (Most likely you'll need to scroll to see them all.) The **Mail** folder holds all your incoming and outgoing mail. To read your mail, select the desired mail message from any folder and click **Open** (alternatively, double-click the message).

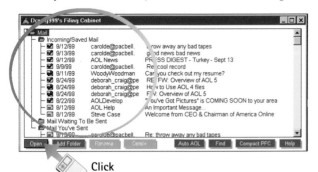

Click

3 Explore the Download Manager

The **Download Manager** folder keeps an informational list of the files you have downloaded or have selected to download. Downloaded files must be opened from the directory to which you downloaded them, usually **C:\America Online 5.0\download**. If you've created any Web pages, the **Web Page** folder contains a list of them (see Part 5 for information on creating Web pages).

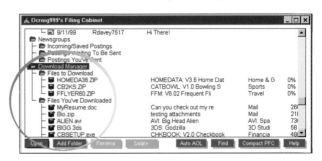

4 Open the Newsgroups Folder

If you've subscribed to any newsgroups, the **Newsgroups** folder holds all your incoming and outgoing newsgroup Automatic AOL messages (newsgroup messages sent and received during Automatic AOL sessions). To read your newsgroup messages, select the message and click **Open** (alternatively, double-click the message). Part 5 describes how to subscribe to newsgroups.

Click

5 Clean Out Your Personal Filing Cabinet

Sooner or later, you will need to remove mail, newsgroup messages, and Download Manager file information from your Personal Filing Cabinet to recover disk space. Select the file or files you want to delete and then press the **Delete** key or click the **Delete** button. When the confirmation window appears, click **Yes** to remove the selected items.

Click

6 Optimizing Your Disk Space

After deleting several items from the Personal Filing Cabinet window, click the **Compact PFC** button to optimize the disk space used by your remaining items. (Doing this helps AOL load more quickly.) The **Performance Warning** window opens; click **Compact Now** to continue. A dialog box informs you when the process is complete. Just click **OK** to proceed.

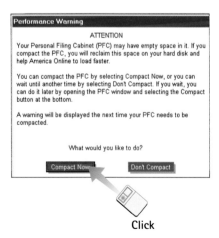

Click

How-To Hints

Using the Find and Add Folder Buttons

In your Personal File Cabinet, use the **Find** button to search through some or all of your folders for keywords. Use the **Add Folder** button to create new folders or subfolders.

Password-Protecting Your PFC

To add a password to your Personal Filing Cabinet, click the **My AOL** button and choose **Preferences;** in the **Preferences** window, click **Passwords**. Enter your password if you haven't already and check the **PFC** check box for your screen name. Now you'll have to enter your password before you can open your Personal Filing Cabinet.

End

How to Set Up Your AOL News Profile

Do you like to keep up with the news but find you're too busy to wade through all the information online? Are you interested in theater or world news, but only certain subjects? AOL has the answer. You can create a news profile that specifies what types of news you want to see, and how much of it. AOL sorts through the news sources you select and delivers articles directly to your mailbox. Each screen name can have more than one news profile but is limited to a maximum of 250 articles per day. Each profile is limited to a maximum of 50 articles per day.

Begin

1 Start a News Profile

Make sure that you're signed on to AOL. Click the **My AOL** icon on the toolbar and select **News Profiles**. The **News Profiles** window opens; use this window as a starting point for creating and managing your news. Click **Create Your News Profiles** to begin setting up a new profile.

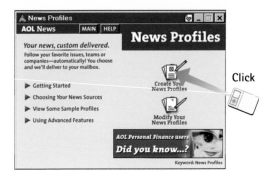

Click

2 Choose a Title and Set Maximum

In the first **News Profiles** window, enter a title in the **Create a title for your news** text box. (You can also use the generic title created by AOL, as shown here.) Adjust the value in the **Limit the number of daily stories** text box to reflect the maximum number of stories you want to receive for this profile each day. Then click **Next**.

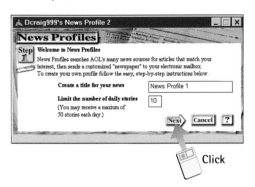

Click

3 Enter Words or Phrases to Find

Specify words or phrases you want to find in articles (not all these words must be present for the article to be selected—just one of them). Enter the words or phrases in the text box, separated by commas, and then click **Next**.

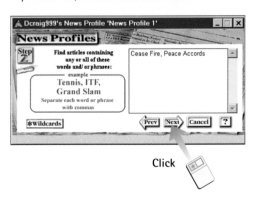

Click

4 Enter Required Words or Phrases

Specify words or phrases that the article *must* contain (the words you enter in this text box must be present for the article to be selected). Again, separate words or phrases by commas. Click **Next** when you're done. In the next window, you can specify words or phrases that you do *not* want to find in articles (if the word is found, you won't receive the article). Click **Next** to move on.

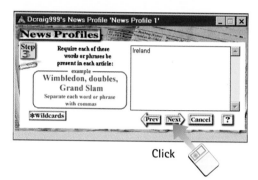

Click

5 Select a News Source

Select the news sources to search for articles that meet your criteria. (AOL provides a wide range of news sources, including Reuters and AP—the Associated Press.) Select a source from the left pane and click **Add** to move it to the right pane. You can add as many sources as you like. If you decide to remove a news source, simply select it from the right pane and click **Remove**. Click **Next** when you're done.

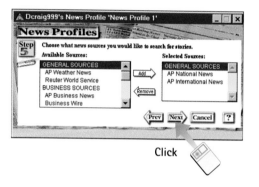

Click

6 Save Your News Profile

Scroll through the **Summary** dialog box to review your selections; if necessary, click the **Prev** button to go back and make changes. When you're satisfied with your selections, click **Done**. A dialog box informs you that your news profile has been created.

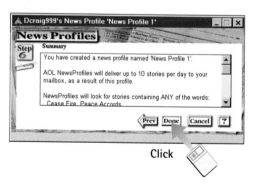

Click

End

How-To Hints

Modifying Existing Profiles

To modify a news profile after it's complete, return to the **News Profile** window shown in Step 1 and click **Modify Your News Profiles**. Then choose the desired profile and click **Edit**. You can also choose a profile and click **Delete** to get rid of it altogether.

Using Wildcards

You can configure your news profile to search for partial words by using asterisks and question marks as wildcards. Use an asterisk to replace zero or more characters (for example, ***ball** would find articles containing **baseball**, **basketball**, **football**, and so on). Use a question mark to replace a single character (for example, **b?ll** would find **ball**, **bell**, **bill**, and **bull**).

How to Set Up an Interest Profile

Interest profiles are new to AOL 5.0. They're similar to news profiles, but instead of focusing on news alone, they let you hone in on AOL areas that match up with your interests. After you set up an interest profile, you'll receive email telling you about AOL sites you might find relevant. The idea is to help you sift through and make sense of the enormous quantity of data that's available on AOL.

Begin

1 Open the Interest Profiles Window

Make sure that you're signed on to AOL. Click the **My AOL** icon on the toolbar and select **Interest Profiles**. The **Interest Profiles** window opens; from here you can create and manage your interest profiles.

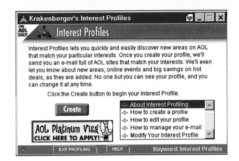

2 Create an Interest Profile

Click the **Create** button to begin setting up an interest profile. (If you've created a profile before, you'll have an **Edit** button instead.) In the first **Interest Profile** window, indicate whether you're a beginning, intermediate, or advanced computer user. When you've made your selection, click **Next** to continue.

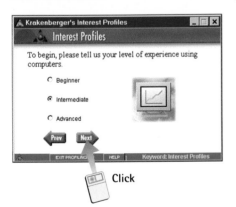

Click

3 Specify Your Interests

In this screen, specify your general interests by clicking any of the check boxes for topics that interest you—anything from games to travel to health. When you're done making your selections, click **Next**.

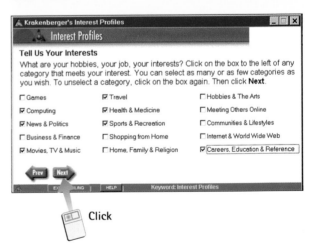

Click

4 Provide Specific Info

In this screen, you are prompted to "get specific" about the general interests you just chose. For example, if you selected **Computing** as an interest, you'll be asked to choose particular computing categories. Double-click each category to select it—a blue arrow appears to the left of its name. (Double-click again to deselect a category.) You can select as many categories as you like. Click **Next** when you're done. The "get specific" screen for the next general topic you selected appears.

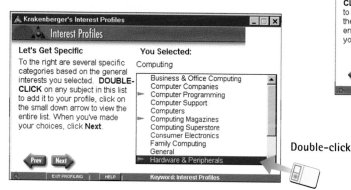

Double-click

5 Finish Getting Specific

Make selections from this screen as you did from the previous one, again clicking **Next** when you're done. Continue this process until you've finished choosing specific categories for all the general areas of interest you selected in Step 3.

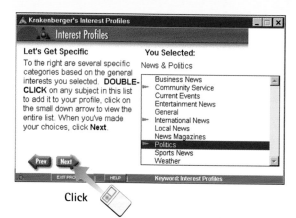

Click

6 Finish Your Interest Profile

After you're done picking categories, you'll see this window, from which you can review your interest profile. If you want, use the **Prev** button to go back and make changes. When your profile seems just right, click **Done**. You'll see a reminder to check your email to find out about AOL areas of interest to you; click **Done** to finish.

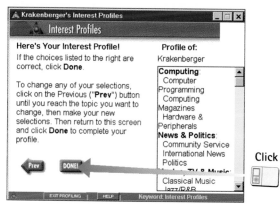

Click

How-To Hints

Turning Off Your Interest Profile Email

Your interest profile works by sending you email to alert you of AOL sites that match your interests. If you decide you no longer want to receive these particular emails (but you *do* want to receive all your other mail), return to the **Interest Profiles** window (click **My AOL** and choose **Interest Profiles**), click **Edit**, and click the **Stop E-Mail** button. Note that if you edit the items in your profile your email will resume, and you'll have to repeat the process described in this hint to stop it again.

End

How to Search a Searchable Database

The fundamentals of searching a searchable database are easy: You type a search criterion and click **List Articles** to see a list of articles that meet your criterion. This type of basic search works well in some circumstances, but isn't efficient in others. For example, if you search AOL's News Search database using the criterion **politics**, AOL might list hundreds of articles, or more. In cases like this, you'll want to narrow your search by using a more-specific criterion or by specifying multiple criteria, as described here.

Begin

1 Search for News

Searchable databases are available all over AOL; in fact, most channels have their own Search area. For this exercise, you'll use a database found in AOL's **News** channel. In the **Welcome** window, click the **News** button; from the **News** channel window, click **Search**. The **News Search** window opens.

Click

2 Use the News Search Window

Type a fairly general criterion in the text box at the top of the search window (such as **space**) and click **List Articles**. You'll see a list of the articles matching that criteria. Note how many matches AOL turned up; this will help you decide whether you need to narrow your search. (By default, only the first 20 articles are listed.

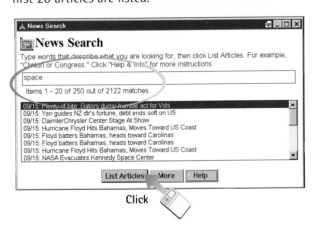

Click

3 Narrow Your Search

If your general criterion produces a short enough list, skip to Step 5. Otherwise, narrow your search by entering multiple search criteria. Type two or more criteria separated by the word **and** to find articles that contain both of those words. You can also precede a word with the word **not** to exclude articles containing that word. After you've modified your search criteria as needed, click **List Articles** again. Repeat this step as necessary to refine your search further.

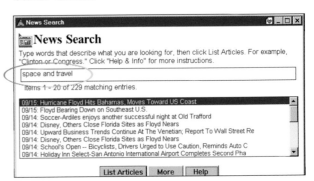

4 Broaden Your Search if Needed

If your criteria narrow your search too much, a dialog box tells you that no matching articles have been found, and you'll have to backtrack and broaden your search. One way of broadening a search is to use the **or** operator. If you type two words separated by **or**, AOL searches for articles containing *either* one or the other of those words. The articles *can* contain both words, but they don't have to.

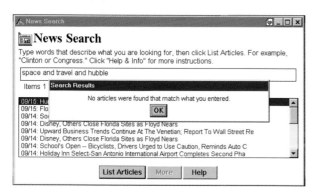

5 Open an Article

After the list shrinks to a manageable size, double-click any article that interests you. A document window showing the article appears.

End

How-To Hints

More About Refining Your Search

As you saw, the words **and**, **or**, and **not** are helpful in refining your search. Use **and** to narrow your search; use **or** to broaden your search to items that match any criteria; use **not** to limit your search to articles that *don't* match a criterion. For example, **dogs and cats** finds articles about both dogs and cats, but not about only one or the other; **dogs or cats** finds articles about dogs, about cats, or about both; **dogs not cats** finds articles about dogs, unless the articles are also about cats. (Incidentally, if you separate two words with a space, that's treated as an **and**.) Yet another way to narrow your search is to enclose phrases within single quotation marks. For instance, entering **'Easter parade'** ensures that you turn up only articles containing that particular phrase, and not articles that just contain the word **Easter** or the word **parade**.

How to Find AOL Members

One of the common problems in a large online community is finding friends and meeting new people with whom you have things in common. Suppose that you know many people who have AOL accounts, and you want to correspond with them by email or check whether they're online so that you can chat. But what if you don't know or can't remember a person's screen name? Fortunately, AOL's **Member Directory** makes it simple to find other members.

Begin

1 Choose AOL Members Directory

Make sure that you're signed on to AOL. Click the **People** button on the toolbar and choose **Search AOL Member Directory**. The **Member Directory** window opens.

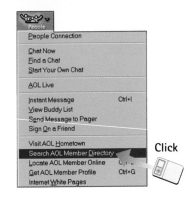

Click

2 Perform a Quick Search

There are two available search methods: Quick Search and Advanced Search. Start with Quick Search. Enter your search criteria in the text boxes (you can enter data in any or all fields). Note that your search words must be at least three characters long. Also notice that you can search not just for names but also for particular words that might appear anywhere in the member's profile.) When you're finished, click **Search**. You'll see the **Member Directory Search Results** window.

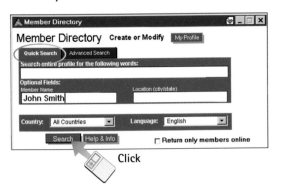

Click

3 Browse the Resulting Member List

This window displays the AOL members who match your search criteria. If the list is too long, continue refining your search in the **Member Directory** window until you come up with a manageable list of names (to return to the **Member Directory** window, click **Cancel** or the close button). For example, you might search for John Smith in Boise, Idaho instead of regular old John Smith. To see a member's personal profile, double-click the screen name. You'll see the **Member Profile** window for the selected member.

Double-click

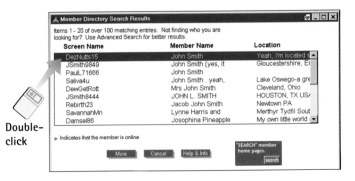

4 View Member Profiles

Profiles are a good way to find information about a person. (From here, you can easily send the member an email or an online greeting just by clicking the appropriate button.) When you're done in the **Member Profile** window, close it by clicking the **Cancel** button or the close button. (You'll learn how to set up your own profile in Part 4, "Chatting.")

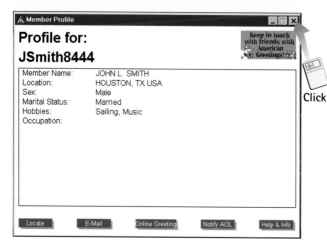

Click

5 Perform an Advanced Search

To search for members with whom you may share interests or common traits, click the **Advanced Search** tab in the **Member Directory** window. Enter keywords in the **Optional Fields** area to search for members who have included those keywords in their personal profiles. You can specify sex, birthday, hobbies, and more. When you're done, click **Search**.

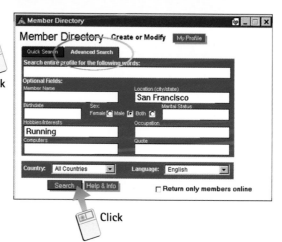

Click

6 Review the Results

The **Member Directory Search Results** window works the same here as it does in the Quick Search; scroll through the list to find people you know or with whom you'd like to get acquainted.

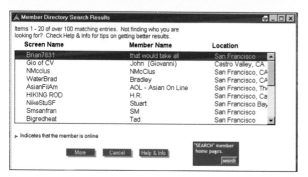

End

How-To Hints

Using Wildcards for Names

If you don't remember the spelling of a person's name, substitute a question mark for any single letter you're unsure of. You can also substitute an asterisk for one or more letters in the person's name.

Using Spaces in Search Criteria

Spaces are not ignored. A space in the search criterion is treated as an **and** operator. (See Task 12 for a description of how the **and** operator works.)

Getting Help with Searches

Click the **Help & Info** button in the **Member Directory** window or the **Member Directory Search Results** window for information about searches.

How to Keep Track of Your Favorites

Remember that cool area you found the other day? Do you have a clue how to get back there? Can't find the keyword for your favorite area? It happens to us all, but there is a solution. Use AOL's Favorites feature. Favorites is your personal list of features and areas you like to visit the most. Any area or feature on AOL—including magazines, clubs, shopping sites, and any place on the Internet—can be part of your Favorites list. After you mark something as a Favorite place, it's easy to get back there with a click or two.

Begin

1 Click the Heart Icon

As you browse through the windows on AOL, notice the heart icon in the upper-right side of the window. You can click this icon to save information about returning to this window.

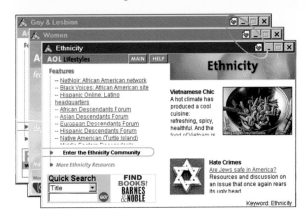

2 Add the Location to Your Favorites

When you click the heart icon, a dialog box opens, asking how you want to use the Favorite Place information. To send the information about this area to someone by email, click **Insert in Mail**. To send an AOL member information about this area in an instant message, click **Insert in Instant Message**. To add this location to your personal Favorites list, click **Add to Favorites**.

3 Return to a Favorite Place

To return to an area you saved in your Favorites list, click the **Favorites** icon in the toolbar and select the menu item for your destination. The window for your destination opens after a moment or two.

Click

4 Choose Favorite Places

If you need to edit your **Favorites** list, click the **Favorites** icon on the toolbar and select **Favorite Places** from the menu. The **Favorite Places** window opens.

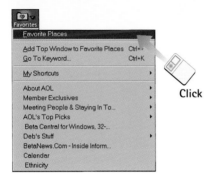

Click

5 Edit Your Favorites

To delete an entry from the **Favorite Places** window, select it and click the **Delete** button. To edit a Favorite Place (change its description or its address), select it and click the **Edit** button. You can also click the **New** button to add new Favorite Places or folders. (To add a new Favorite place, make sure that the **New Favorite Place** radio button is selected and then enter a description and an Internet address for the place. To add a new folder, make sure that the **New Folder** radio button is selected and enter a folder description.) Finally, you can go directly to a Favorite by selecting it and clicking **Go**.

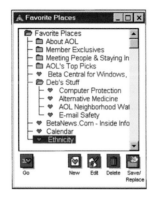

6 Save Your Favorites

The **Favorite Places** window offers a new option that can be handy if you've organized a whole slew of favorites into folders and then want to move them to another computer. Click the **Save/Replace** button in the **Favorite Places** window. Then choose **Save the Favorite Places for your current screen name** and click **OK**; in the **Save Folder** dialog box that opens, choose where to save your Favorite Places file. Later, when you want to retrieve this Favorite Places file, choose **Save/Replace** again, but this time select **Replace the Favorite Places for your current screen name**, and choose the name of the Favorite Places file you saved. (If you're moving to a different computer, you can save the file to and retrieve it from a floppy disk.)

How-To Hints

Reorganizing Your Favorites

To reorganize your Favorite Places, open the **Favorite Places** window and drag the heart icons to new locations in the directory tree. Creating new folders (as described in Step 5) can help you get organized. You can, for example, create a new Favorite Places folder called **Health**, and then drag all your health-related Favorite Places into that folder.

You can also add your favorite Internet sites to your Favorites list. To do this, click the **Favorites** toolbar icon and choose **Favorite Places**. In the resulting dialog box, enter a description of the site and the site's URL (Internet address). Make sure that you enter the URL correctly or the link won't work.

End

How to Set Up My Places

My Places, on the newly spiffed-up AOL 5.0 **Welcome** window, is another way of placing some of your "favorite places" at your fingertips. You can choose from a large list of some of the most popular online destinations, and display them right on your **Welcome** screen for easy access. And if you discover that you don't go to your chosen places very often, or that you simply want to expand your horizons to incorporate new places, it's just as easy to change what's displayed under **My Places**.

Begin

1 Display the Welcome Window

Make sure that you're signed on to AOL and that your **Welcome** window is open and visible.

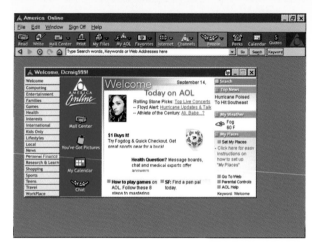

2 Choose My Places

Click **My Places**; it's on the right side of the **Welcome** window. The **Change My Places** window opens. You use this screen to specify AOL areas that interest you.

Click

3 Change Your Places

Click the **Choose New Place** button to the left of the number **1**. A menu of interest categories drops down.

Click

4 Choose Your First New Place

Choose a category—such as **Health** or **Travel**—and then choose a subcategory from the resulting submenu—such as **Medical Reference** or **Airline Reservations**. The area you select will appear under **My Places** on your **Welcome** screen.

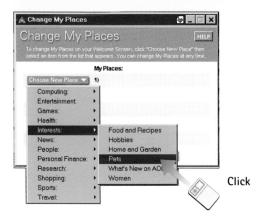

Click

5 Create Additional New Places

Repeat Steps 3 and 4 to select up to five topics to appear under **My Places**: Click the **Choose New Place** button next to the number **2**, **3**, **4**, or **5** and choose another area of interest.

Click

6 Saving the My Places Selections

After you've assigned topics to as many of the **Choose New Place** buttons as you like, save your selections by clicking the **Save My Changes** button. You'll see this message: **The items you have just selected are now saved**. The items will appear in the **My Places** area on your **Welcome** screen. When you click **OK**, you'll see your changes on the **Welcome** screen and can travel to those places just by clicking their links.

Click

End

How-To Hints

Overwriting Earlier My Places Selections

The process described in this task works the same whether you're defining **My Places** for the very first time or overwriting some settings you made earlier.

Canceling Your Changes

Suppose that you've already set up **My Places** and are making modifications to these settings in the **Change My Places** window. If you change your mind, you can easily go back to your original selections by clicking the **Cancel Changes** button. This action both wipes out any new settings you've chosen and closes the **Change My Places** window.

How to Find Billing Information

With AOL, as with other services such as your telephone, billing is an unavoidable issue. If you have a question about billing—whether it's about how to change your address or what billing plans you can choose from—AOL's **Accounts & Billing** section can help answer your questions. Most of the activities for taking care of billing changes have been automated so that you can easily make the changes yourself. Even though you still have to pay your bills, being able to get to the information you need easily and quickly should be something of a consolation.

Begin

1 Update Your Info

Make sure that you're signed on to AOL. Choose **Help, Accounts and Billing**. The **AOL Billing Center** window opens. Note that on the left are options for updating your personal information as well as for updating your billing method or price plan.

2 View Your Bill

Under **View Your Bill** are several options for looking at your current bill. Click **Display Your Detailed Bill** to see information on the use of your account. Choose either **Current Months Bill** or **Last Months Bill** to see a window of information something like the one shown here. This window shows the screen names in your account and indicates the amount of time used by the various people each time they logged in to AOL.

Time On	Name	Free	Paid	Charge	Credit	Total
99-09-15 02:03	Dcraig999	1	4	0.00	0.00	0.00
99-09-15 00:39	Dcraig999	0	77	0.00	0.00	0.00
99-09-14 02:57	Dcraig999	0	38	0.00	0.00	0.00
99-09-12 14:06	Dcraig999	0	34	0.00	0.00	0.00
99-09-11 23:07	Dcraig999	0	147	0.00	0.00	0.00
99-09-11 19:54	Dcraig999	1	71	0.00	0.00	0.00
99-09-11 19:53	WoodyWoodman	0	2	0.00	0.00	0.00
99-09-11 19:50	Dcraig999	0	3	0.00	0.00	0.00
99-09-11 19:49	WoodyWoodman	0	2	0.00	0.00	0.00
99-09-11 19:47	Dcraig999	0	2	0.00	0.00	0.00
99-09-11 19:45	WoodyWoodman	0	2	0.00	0.00	0.00
99-09-11 17:05	Dcraig999	0	160	0.00	0.00	0.00
••••••••••••••	Total	2	542	0.00	0.00	0.00
•••••••••••••• 0.00	Total	2	542	0.00	0.00	

Print A Copy   Cancel

3 Investigate the FAQs

Return to the **AOL Billing Center** window and notice the series of FAQs (Frequently Asked Questions) on the right side of the window. These links provide answers to some of the most commonly asked questions by AOL members. To experiment, click **What pricing plans does AOL offer?** to display a Help screen of relevant information.

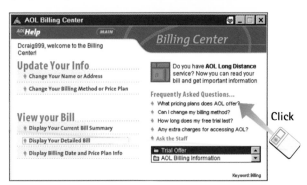

Click

4 The Five Pricing Plans

Click the first blue and underlined word **here** to find out more about AOL's five pricing plans. (As you may already know, words that are blue and underlined are links that will lead you to more information.) The **Review Price Plans** window opens.

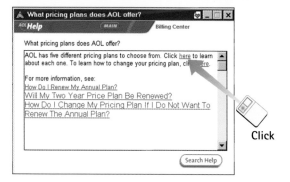

Click

5 The Unlimited Monthly Plan

Click the **Unlimited Monthly** button to read up on this particular payment plan—a popular one for those who want unlimited usage, as opposed to having to pay per time on line. If you want to read about other pricing plans, close the **Standard Unlimited Plan** window (click its close button) and choose another pricing plan from the **Review Price Plans** window.

Click

6 Find More FAQs

Close any open windows until you return to the **AOL Billing Center** window. From here, you can delve into additional FAQs by clicking their links or by choosing them from the list box in the lower-right corner of the window.

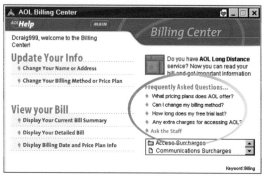

End

How-To Hints

What's Your Billing Plan?

If you're not sure what billing plan you're on, open the **AOL Billing Center** window and click the **Display Billing Date and Price Plan Info** link in the lower-left corner of the window.

Changing Your Billing

It is possible to change your billing method and pricing plan online. However, you must enter your password before you can do so. This procedure is simple: from the **AOL Billing Center** window, click **Change Your Billing Method or Price Plan**. Enter your password and click **Continue**. Then choose whether you want to update your billing method or pricing plan.

How to Use My Calendar

You can use AOL 5's new **My Calendar** feature to keep track of your appointments, to note special occasions such as birthdays and anniversaries, and to search for events in AOL's **Event Directory** (adding them to your calendar if they strike your fancy). You can even get your horoscope or determine what the weather will be on a particular date.

Begin

1 Register for My Calendar

Click the **My Calendar** button in the **Welcome** window. The first time you use **My Calendar**, you have to register. Choose a time zone and enter your zip code (so that **My Calendar** can find events close to you). Then click the **Save** button.

Click

2 Navigate My Calendar

My Calendar has three tabs—**Calendar**, **Event Directory**, and **Help & Tour**. In the **Calendar** tab, you can also click the **Day**, **Week**, and **Month** tabs at the bottom of the screen to get anything from a big picture (monthly) to a close-up (daily) view of your calendar. To switch to the next or previous month, week, or day, click the left (previous) and right (next) arrows to the right of the month, week, or day designation at the top of the calendar.

Click here to display the previous month

Click here to display the next month

3 Enter Appointments

Click the **Calendar** tab. Click the **Add** button at the top of the calendar. In the **Appointment Details** window that opens, enter a title, date, and time for your appointment. Select **No Specific Time** to mark a day—such as an anniversary—without scheduling an event for a particular time. Click the **Save** button when you're done. (Click **Save & Add Another** to generate another appointment.) The appointment shows up on your calendar.

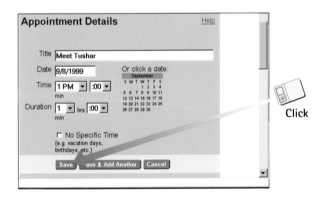

Click

4 Enter Repeating Appointments

You can also enter repeating appointments to remind yourself of a monthly meeting or a special birthday or anniversary. Start by setting up an appointment as described in Step 3. Then scroll down to the **Repeat** area at the bottom of the **Appointment Details** window. Select the **Repeats** radio button and specify whether this appointment repeats every day, week, year, or month. You can also set the appointment to repeat **every other**, **every 3rd**, or **every 4th** day, month, year, and so on. Select the **Repeats on the** radio button to repeat events on the first, second, third, fourth, or last Sunday, Monday, Tuesday, and so on. To end such repeating appointments at a particular time, specify a date to the right of the **End by** option button. Click **Save** when you're done.

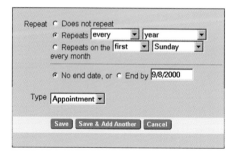

6 Add Events to Your Calendar

If you find an event you want to attend, you can add it to your calendar. Just click the check box to the left of each event you want to attend. If you're viewing a list, click the **Add** button to add all checked events to your calendar; if you're looking at the weekly or monthly view, click the **Add checked events to your calendar** button. Note that adding an event to your calendar *does not* actually reserve you a ticket for the event; it simply notes the day and time of the event in your calendar as a reminder.

End

5 Explore the Event Directory

Click the **Event Directory** tab in **My Calendar**. Here you can find lists of events—movies, concerts, sports events, and more—that might grab your interest. Click an event category (for this example, click **Concerts**). From the next screen, choose a venue (mostly these are states) or a metropolitan area in which to search (for example, you may want to hunt for concerts in San Francisco). When you find a concert you're interested in, click it to read more about it.

Click

How-To Hints

Sending Email Notifications

You can have relevant people notified by email when you create or modify an appointment. To do this, create or edit an appointment. In the **Appointment Details** window, scroll down to the **Email Attendees** area and enter the email addresses of all appropriate people (separate addresses with commas).

Editing and Deleting Appointments

Calendars almost always need revising at some point. Luckily, it's easy to edit and delete appointments. Just find the appointment in your calendar and click it. In the **Appointment Details** window, click the **Delete** button to kill the appointment. To modify the appointment, make any needed changes and click the **Save** button.

How to Use You've Got Pictures

One of AOL's coolest and most vivid new features is **You've Got Pictures**. Just take your film to a participating photo developer and check the **AOL** box on the film processing envelope to have your photos delivered to your AOL account. When your pictures are ready, you'll be notified when you log on (you'll get an email and, if you have audio, a voice will say "You've got pictures"). (Unfortunately, because **You've Got Pictures** is so new, it is only available in certain areas.)

Begin

1 Find a Photo Developer

The first step is to take your film to a participating photo developer. To find one, click the **You've Got Pictures** button on the **Welcome** window. In the resulting **You've Got Pictures Quick Start** window, make sure that the **#1 Drop Off Film** tab is selected; click the **Click here** link. When prompted, enter your zip code and click **Send**. Soon you'll receive an email with a list of nearby photo developers.

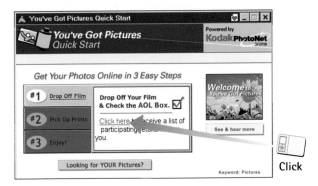

2 Retrieve Your Pictures

When your photos ready, you'll receive an email notification from **AOL YouveGotPics**. To retrieve your pictures, click **You've Got Pictures** on the **Welcome** window. The **My Pictures** window opens. The **New Rolls** tab lists the title of your roll, the number of pictures it contains, and its expiration date. (To keep photos for the long term, you must save or download them before this date.) If you have multiple rolls, select the radio button for the roll you want to look at.

Click

3 View Your Pictures

To look over the pictures in the selected roll, click the **View** button. The **Roll Viewer** window opens, which includes small renditions of all the photos in your roll. To look at individual pictures at full size, click the small image. The **Full Picture** window opens. Click the **Next Picture** or **Previous Picture** button to look at the next or previous picture in the roll.

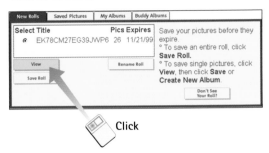

Click

4 Email a Picture to a Friend

From either the **Full Picture** or the **Roll Viewer** window, you can send individual photos to your friends and family with email: simply click the **E-mail Picture** button (if you're in the **Roll Viewer** window, first select which photo you want to send). In the **E-mail a Picture** dialog box, type the name of the recipient or recipients, type a message, and click **Send**. If you want to send more than a single picture, you must put together a photo album, as described next.

Click

5 Create a Photo Album

Photo albums let you organize your photos into groups. To create an album, return to the **Roll Viewer** window, click the check boxes for the pictures you want to include in the album, and click **Create New Album**. Click the **Customize** button to add new pictures to the album, give the album a title, add photo captions, or change the album's background color. Click **Save** when you're done. To share the album with others, go to the **My Albums** tab in the **My Pictures** window, select the desired album, click the **Share** button, and specify the appropriate email addresses.

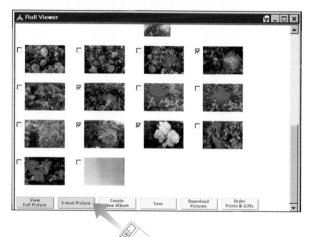

Click

6 Save Your Photos

New rolls don't remain on the **New Rolls** tab indefinitely; they expire about a month after being processed. To keep your photos more permanently, you must either download them or save them on AOL. (Note that when you create an album, the photos you place in it are saved automatically.) When you save photos on AOL, they appear in the **Saved Pictures** tab of the **My Pictures** window. (You can save up to 50 pictures here for free; if you want to save more, you can pay for the additional storage space.) To save selected pictures, select the pictures to save in the **Roll Viewer** window and click **Save**. To download pictures to your hard drive, select the pictures and click **Download Pictures**.

End

How-To Hints

Ordering Personalized Stuff Online

The **You've Got Pictures** feature also lets you take a photographic shopping spree. Among other things, you can order mugs, puzzles, sweatshirts, T-shirts, and mouse pads with your pictures on them. These items make great gifts or treats for yourself. Click the **Order Prints & Gifts** button (the button is available in multiple places, including the **Full Picture** window, the **Roll Viewer** window, and the **Saved Pictures** tab of the **My Pictures** window).

Task

Communicating

AOL's online service is a great place to meet people and communicate your ideas and opinions. In these tasks, you learn three ways to communicate. First you'll find out how to use AOL's electronic mail (also known as email) features. Email is an invaluable way to keep in touch with friends, family, and co-workers. Next you'll see how to send Instant Messages to both AOL members and your friends on the Internet. If the person you want to talk to is online, Instant Messages appear on his or her screen almost immediately after you send them. Finally, you'll learn about message boards, which are similar to the cork-and-pushpin message boards you see in many grocery stores, libraries, and Laundromats. Message boards offer places for people to openly post messages for other AOL members to read.

AOL also lets you communicate in a number of additional ways, such as with chat rooms, newsgroups, and mailing lists. You'll learn about these features in Parts 4 and 5. ●

How to Send Mail

Composing and sending email (or *mail*) to other AOL members and Internet users is easy. You type a message just as you would to send it by traditional mail, but instead of going through the bother of printing the message, addressing an envelope, and running down to the corner mailbox, you just click a few onscreen buttons. You don't even have to find or lick any stamps. Better yet, the price is the same whether you're sending your message down the hallway or around the world.

Begin

1 Choose the Write Icon

Make sure that you're signed on to AOL. Click the **Write** icon on the toolbar. (You can also press **Ctrl+M** or choose **Write Mail** from the **Mail Center** menu.) The **Write Mail** window opens. Incidentally, you can also compose email messages while you're offline and send them later—a great strategy if you want to minimize your time online.

Click

2 Enter a Screen Name or Email Address

In the **Send To** list box, type the recipient's screen name or Internet mail address. (If you want to type several addresses, separate them with commas.) It doesn't matter if you type the address in uppercase, lowercase, or a mixture of the two.

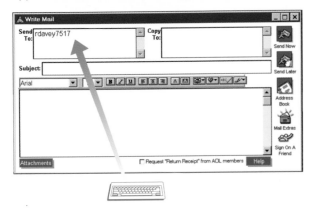

3 Send Carbon Copies

If you want to send a *carbon copy* of your message to another person, type his or her address in the **Copy To** list box. (To specify several recipients, separate their email addresses with commas.) To send a *blind carbon copy*, type the address in the **Copy To** list box and enclose it within parentheses. (Other recipients of the message won't be able to see that this person also received the message.)

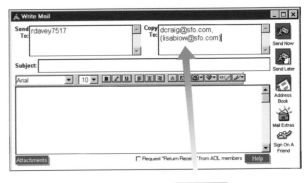

4 Type a Subject and Message

Type a subject for your message in the **Subject** box. Your recipients see this text before opening your message, so it's best to make the subject concise and descriptive. In the large box at the bottom of the window, type your message. Use the arrow, **Backspace**, and **Delete** keys to review and edit the message. When you finish addressing and composing your message, click **Send Now** to send it right away.

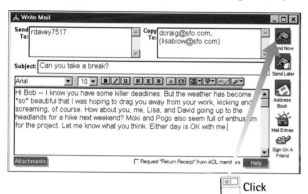

Click

5 Close the Confirmation Dialog Box

If all is well, a dialog box will inform you that your mail has been sent. Click **OK** to close this dialog box.

Click

6 Unsending Messages

If you send a message and then have a change of heart, you *might* be able to unsend it. (The two catches are that the recipient must be an AOL member and must not have read the message yet.) Click the **Mail Center** toolbar icon and choose **Sent Mail**. (If you're already in your mailbox, just click the **Sent Mail** tab.) In the list of recently sent messages, highlight the message or messages you want to unsend and click the **Unsend** button. Click **Yes** when asked if you're sure you want to unsend the message.

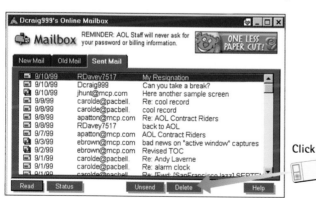

Click

End

How-To Hints

Finding Screen Names

If you're unsure of a recipient's screen name, try finding it in AOL's Member Directory, as described in Part 2, Task 13, "How to Find AOL Members." If this doesn't work for some reason, consider telephoning your friend to get his or her screen name.

Internet Email Addresses

Internet email addresses are always in the format **user@company.name**. It's probably easiest to ask for a person's Internet email address or to have that person send you an email message so that you can read the email address in the message's **From** line. If you're an AOL member, your Internet email address is your screen name, minus any spaces, followed by **@aol.com** (for example, if your screen name is **dcraig999**, your Internet email address is **dcraig999@aol.com**). Someone who's on AOL can just email you using your screen name; someone who's not on AOL must send you email at your Internet address.

How to Read Mail You Receive

One of the coolest things about sending mail is that it greatly increases your chances of receiving mail in return. If you've been an AOL member for more that a day or so, you have probably already received a mail message from AOL President Steve Case, welcoming you to the service. If you've successfully read this message, you know the basics of reading mail; check out this task to learn a little more. And if your mail has been piling up because you aren't sure how to look at it, this section will get you going.

Begin

1 How to Tell if You Have Mail

Whenever you're online, look at the **Read** icon on the toolbar. If the mailbox is open with a letter showing, you've got new mail waiting. If the mailbox is closed, you have no new mail. If you don't have mail, you'll either have to find someone to send you mail or send some mail to yourself just for testing purposes.

 —You've got mail

 —No new mail

2 Open Your Mailbox

Click the **Read** icon to open your mailbox. (You can also press **Ctrl+R** or choose **Read Mail** from the **Mail Center** menu.) An **Online Mailbox** window opens, displaying a list of all the mail messages you've received but haven't yet read. Select the message you want to look at and click **Read**. (Or double-click the message in the list.)

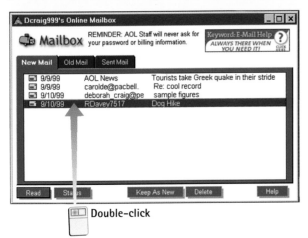

Double-click

3 Read the Selected Message

The mail message opens in its own window. Scroll as necessary to read the message. (To keep a permanent copy of the message, you can save or print it. To print, make sure that the message is open and then click the **Print** icon on the toolbar or press **Ctrl+P**. To save messages, read the next task.)

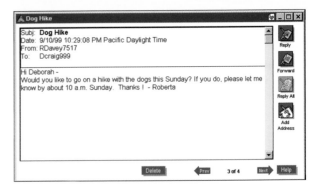

4 Read Additional Messages

If you have more than one mail message waiting, a **Next** button appears at the bottom of the message window. Click this button to display the next message. Repeat this step as necessary to read all your mail. (You can also click the **Prev** button to read previous messages.) When you're done reading messages, click the message window's close box (the × in the title bar) to return to the **Online Mailbox** window.

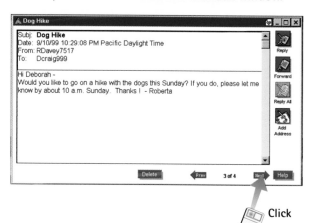

Click

6 Read Old or Sent Mail

The **Old Mail** (or **Sent Mail**) window opens with a list of messages that you've either already read or sent. Select the message you want to review and click **Read**. The message opens in its own window, as shown in Step 3.

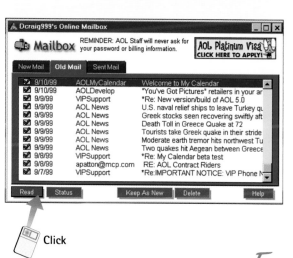

Click

End

5 Review Old and Sent Mail

From the **Online Mailbox** window, you can review mail you've already read by clicking the **Old Mail** tab. You can look over mail you've sent by clicking the **Sent Mail** tab.

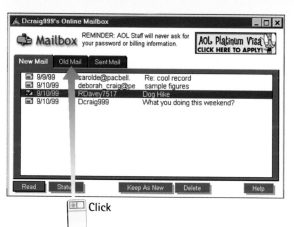

Click

How-To Hints

Replying to Email

It's easy to reply to an email message you've just read—just click the **Reply** button. (If the message was sent to several people at once, a **Reply All** button lets you reply to all the recipients at once, as opposed to just the sender.) A **Write Mail** window opens. The **To** and **Subject** lines are filled in automatically; all you have to do is type your message and click **Send Now**.

Deleting Messages

If you receive a mail message you know you'd rather not read, select the message in the **Online Mailbox** window and then click **Delete**. The message is permanently removed. (In other words, do this with caution.)

The Keep As New Button

The **Keep As New** button in the **New Mail** and **Old Mail** windows enables you to mark a read message as unread so that it will remain in the **New Mail** area of the mailbox.

How to Retrieve Mail Remotely

Do you go through withdrawal when you can't get your email? You don't necessarily have to be at your own computer to retrieve your AOL mail. Using any computer with AOL installed, you can log in as a **Guest** user and check out your own email. This technique works whether you're across the street or on a different continent. If the computer you're using does not have AOL installed, you should still be able to tap into your email account by using AOL Mail, as described in Task 12, later in this part.

Begin

1 Launch AOL

Launch AOL as usual: double-click the desktop shortcut, choose the AOL icon from the taskbar, or use any other favorite method. The **Sign On** window opens.

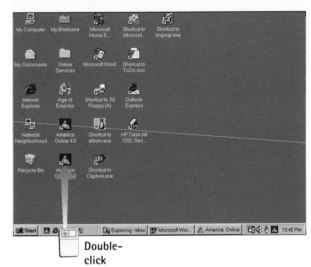

Double-click

2 Sign On as Guest

Choose **Guest** from the **Select Screen Name** drop-down list box. Then click the **Sign On** button. The **Guest Sign-On** dialog box opens.

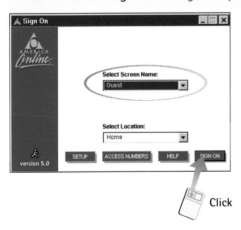

Click

3 Enter Screen Name and Password

Type your AOL screen name and password and then click **OK**.

Click

4 Read Your Email

After you're logged on, you can read your email as you usually do. (You'll know whether you have mail if you hear the cheery voice say "You've got mail" and if there's a letter in the mailbox icon.) Check the instructions in the preceding task if you need to refresh your memory.

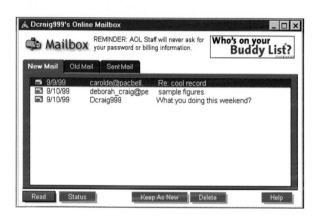

5 Reply to Email Remotely

When you're logged on as a guest, you can reply to your mail too. Just open your mail messages as usual, click the **Reply** button, type your response, and click **Send Now**. (There's also nothing to stop you from sending new messages, as described in Task 1, "How to Send Mail.")

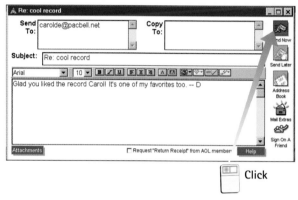

Click

End

How-To Hints

What You Can't Do As a Guest User

There are a few drawbacks to logging in as a guest: You won't be able to use your Address Book, your Personal Filing Cabinet, or your list of Favorite Places. (These personalized features all "live" on your own computer.) You also won't be able to use the Download Manager or Automatic AOL.

Dialing in to AOL from the Road

If you're on the road with a laptop computer, you can check your AOL email without racking up long-distance charges: Just use a local access number. In the **Sign On** screen, click **Access Numbers,** type your current (local) area code, select an access number, and click **Next** to dial in using that number. If you have to delete those numbers later, click **Setup** in the **Sign On** screen, click **Edit AOL access phone numbers or change dialing order**, and make any required changes.

How to Retrieve Recently Deleted Mail

Email is so easy to send that we sometimes receive too much of it—whether it's work correspondence, casual greetings, Internet jokes from friends, or electronic junk mail. If you're like me, you may have to delete email just as fast as it comes in strictly for self-preservation. But then you run the risk of un-intentionally deleting something you'd actually like to keep. If this happens, and you change your mind quickly enough, AOL 5.0 lets you retrieve recently deleted mail.

Begin

1 Delete a Mail Message

If you haven't deleted an email message or two in the last 24 hours, delete something now. (Just go into your mailbox, select a message, and click the **Delete** button.)

Click

2 Display Recently Deleted Mail

Click the **Mail Center** icon on the tool-bar and choose **Recently Deleted Mail** from the menu that appears. The **Recently Deleted Mail** window opens, showing a list of all the mail you've deleted within the last 24 hours.

Click

3 Read Recently Deleted Mail

If you want to read a deleted message, double-click that message in the list or select it and click the **Read** button. The message opens in a separate window, just as you've come to expect.

Double-click

4 Read Additional Deleted Messages

You can read through all your recently deleted emails by using the **Next** and **Prev** buttons at the bottom of the read window, much as you read your ordinary email. When you're done reading through deleted emails, you can close the message window by clicking its close button.

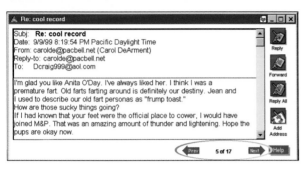

5 Restore a Deleted Message

You can "undelete" a deleted message by selecting it in the **Recently Deleted Mail** window and clicking the **Keep As New** button. This **Keep As New** button works just like the button by the same name in the **Online Mailbox** window: It transfers the message back to the **New Mail** tab in your **Online Mailbox**.

Click

6 Killing Messages Forever

If you're sure that you want to get rid of a message for good, you can click the **Permanently Delete** button in the **Recently Deleted Mail** window. *Be careful with this button!* After you use it, you have no way of getting that message back.

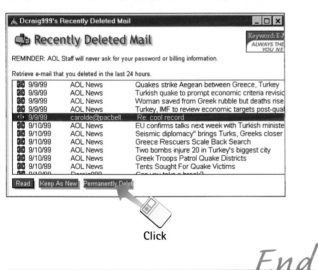

Click

End

How-To Hints

Delete Email with Care

The **Recently Deleted Mail** feature is similar to the **Unsend** feature. It can come in *very* handy, but only if you use it in time. (The **Unsend** feature works only if the mail hasn't been read yet; the **Recently Deleted Mail** feature works only within a 24-hour window.) In other words, **Recently Deleted Mail** is a convenient new feature but it's no substitute for thinking very carefully before you delete email messages.

Finding Restored Email

Suppose that you thought you had restored a recently deleted email with the **Keep As New** button, but now can't find it in your Online Mailbox? Try closing the Online Mailbox window and then reopening it. This time, you should see the undeleted email.

How to Store Mail on Your Computer

As you use mail more and more, you'll undoubtedly need to refer to a message you've sent or received. Because AOL regularly removes the mail you've read and sent, take advantage of AOL's option to save mail to your computer. Messages will then be stored in your Personal Filing Cabinet (see Part 2, "America Online Features," for more information on using your Personal Filing Cabinet) so that you can open and reread your mail anytime, without even having to be online.

Begin

1 Set Your Preferences

Click the **My AOL** icon in the toolbar and select **Preferences** from the **My AOL** menu. You don't need to be online to set up mail preferences. The **Preferences** window opens.

2 Choose Mail

Click the **Mail** icon to open the **Mail Preferences** dialog box.

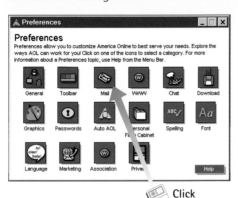

3 Set Your Mail Preferences

Several items in the **Mail Preferences** dialog box will already be selected. AOL sets up these items by default, but you can change them any time. Select **Retain all mail I send in my Personal Filing Cabinet** or **Retain all mail I read in my Personal Filing Cabinet**. When these options are selected, AOL saves your mail for you automatically, enabling you to refer back to it later. After you've selected the desired features, click **OK**.

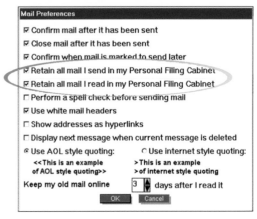

4 Open Your Personal Filing Cabinet

The next time you want to review mail you've read or sent, click the **My Files** icon and choose **Personal Filing Cabinet**. (Note that you need not be online to do this.) The **Filing Cabinet** window opens.

Click

5 Read Your Mail

To review mail you've read, double-click the **Incoming/Saved Mail** folder. To review mail you've sent, double-click the **Mail You've Sent** folder. In either folder, select the message you want to read and click **Open** to view the message.

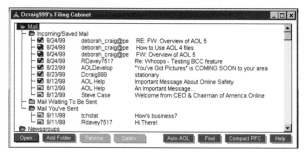

End

How-To Hints

Another Way of Saving

Any mail you've received or sent before you check the **Retain Mail** check boxes won't be saved in your Personal Filing Cabinet. If you need to save these messages, select the message in your Online Mailbox window and select **File, Save**. You'll have to give a location and name to the files you're saving. You can store them anywhere on your hard drive—preferably in some place you'll remember how to find your way back to later.

Select Your Screen Name First

There's a different Personal Filing Cabinet associated with each screen name you have set up on your computer. For this reason, make sure that *your* screen name appears in the **Select Screen Name** box on the **Sign On** or **Goodbye** window before you open your Personal Filing Cabinet. See Part 6, "Sharing America Online with Your Family," for the scoop on setting up additional screen names and switching among them.

Preferences Apply to Master and Subaccounts

The **Retain all mail I send** and **Retain all mail I read** preferences—that is, the preferences having to do with mail you're keeping and mail you've sent out—apply to your primary account (the one you joined AOL with) and any subaccounts (alternative screen names) you may have. Again, consult Part 6 for the lowdown on using multiple screen names with a single account.

How to Attach a File to Mail

You probably use many programs on your computer, such as a word processor or a spreadsheet program. You've most likely also had to share a document or spreadsheet with a friend or colleague. The next time you want to share a file, don't copy it to a floppy disk and deliver it to your friend; instead, attach the file to a mail message. When you send your message, the file is sent along with it. After the message reaches its destination, it's a fairly simple task for the recipient to copy the file (that is, to *download* the file) to his or her own computer.

Begin

1 Compose a Message

Compose a mail message as you normally would. (For details, refer to Task 1, "How to Send Mail," earlier in this part.) In the message, explain the purpose of the file that you'll be attaching, and then click the **Attachments** button. The **Attachments** dialog box opens.

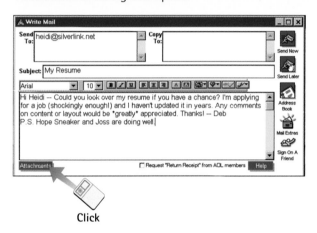

Click

2 Open the Attach Dialog Box

Click **Attach** to open the **Attach** dialog box.

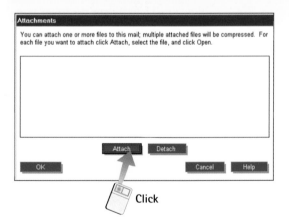

Click

3 Find the File to Attach

Identify where the file you want to attach is stored on your computer. (If you need help locating files, consult your Windows documentation.) Click the file in the list box and click **Open**.

Click

4 Attaching the File

When the **Attach** dialog box closes, notice that the name of the selected file appears in the **Attachments** window. (If you change your mind about the attached file, click the **Detach** button.) To attach multiple files to a single email message, repeat Steps 2 through 4 for each file. Click **OK** to return to the **Write Mail** window.

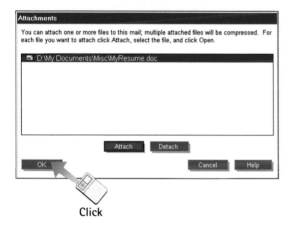

Click

5 Send a Message and Attachment

Note that the name of the attached file is listed to the right of the **Attachments** button. When the message is completed to your satisfaction, click **Send Now**.

Click

6 The File Transfer

A **File Transfer** dialog box charts the progress of the file transfer from your computer to AOL. The length of this transfer depends primarily on the file's size and your modem's speed. After the file transfer is complete, another dialog box informs you that the file transfer is complete. (And the cheery voice pipes in to say "file's done.") Your message and the file have now been sent. Click **OK** to close this dialog box.

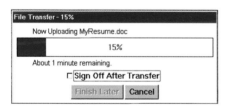

End

How-To Hints

Uploading and Downloading

The words *uploading* and *downloading* describe the two directions of file transfers. Uploading is the process of transferring files from your computer to another computer. Downloading is the process of transferring files from another computer to your computer. For more information on uploading and downloading files from AOL, see Part 2.

Compressing Files

As you learned in Task 6, "How to Upload a File," in Part 2, it's wise to compress files before uploading them. The same holds true for attachments; attached files transfer more speedily if you compress them first. However, if you're attaching multiple files, you don't need to worry about compressing them because AOL does this for you—it both compacts them and stashes them together in a single file for convenience.

How to Read an Attached File

The previous task explained how to send files as attachments. This feature makes it easy to exchange files with friends and co-workers. When you receive an email message that includes an attached file, you can't just read that file from within AOL. Instead, you must typically view it in the program that it was created with in the first place—whether that's Word or Photoshop. AOL makes it easy to "detach" and download these files.

Begin

1 Open an Attached File

Open your mail messages as you normally would. (For details, refer to the Task 2, "How to Read Mail You Receive.") When you open a message that has a file attached, the message lists the filename and its size as well as the estimated time for downloading. To transfer the attached file from AOL to your computer, click the **Download Now** button.

Click

2 Choose a Location

You may see a warning message about downloading attachments; make sure that the attachment is from a trusted source before clicking **Yes** to proceed. In the **Download Manager** dialog box, decide where you want to place the file. (By default, AOL places downloaded files in your **Download** directory within your America Online directory.) Click **Save** to start the download.

Click

3 Begin the Transfer

A **File Transfer** dialog box opens to chart the progress of your file transfer; it also indicates the approximate time remaining until the transfer is complete.

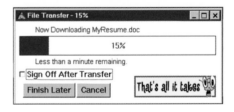

4 Confirm the Transfer

After the file transfer is complete, a dialog box opens to inform you of that fact. (And the familiar cheery voice chimes in with "file's done.") Click the **OK** button to close this dialog box.

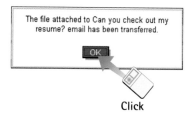

Click

5 Open the Downloaded File

To view the downloaded file, open Windows Explorer. (For more information, check your Windows documentation.) Open the appropriate folders (directories) to locate your file, and double-click the file to open it.

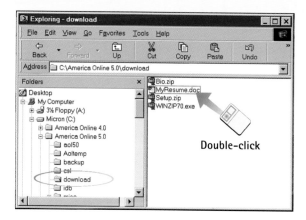

Double-click

6 View the Downloaded File

The file opens in the program with which it was created. (If the file has been zipped—that is, compressed—you'll have to unzip it before you can use it. See Part 2, Task 6, "How to Upload a File," for details on finding a compression program.)

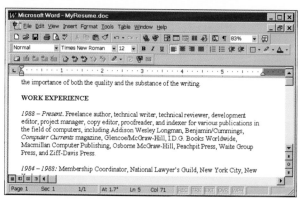

How-To Hints

Make Sure That You Have the Right Software

Before trying to open the transferred file, make sure that you have the program that was used to create it. If you're not sure which program you need, try opening the file by double-clicking it. The necessary program may launch automatically. If not, you'll be given the opportunity to choose which program to open the file with.

A List of Downloaded Files

A list of the files you've downloaded is available in your Personal Filing Cabinet. In the **Download Manager** folder, open the **Files You've Downloaded** folder. For information on any of the downloaded files, right-click the item and choose **Show Status** from the context menu that appears. You'll see information including the filename and the directory in which you saved the file.

How to Use the Address Book

Like postal addresses, email addresses (AOL screen names and Internet addresses) can be difficult to remember. Although you could maintain a paper list of email addresses, a better option is to take advantage of AOL's Address Book. The Address Book enables you to maintain an electronic list of your online correspondents' real names and email addresses. The Address Book can also help you easily and accurately address your mail messages.

Begin

1 Open the Address Book

Open a **Write Mail** window as you normally would to start composing a mail message. (For details, refer to Task 1, "How to Send Mail," earlier in this part.) Rather than typing an email address in the **Send To** or **Copy To** text box, click **Address Book**. The **Address Book** window opens.

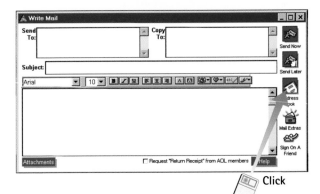

Click

2 Start a New Address

If you haven't entered any addresses yet, the **Address Book** window should be empty. To start creating an address entry for an individual, click **New Person**. A **New Person** dialog box opens.

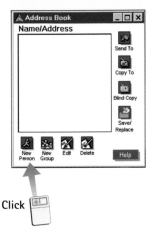

Click

3 Enter Address Information

Fill out the text boxes with the first and last names and email address of your contact. (The email address can be an AOL or an Internet address.) The **Notes** text box is for any additional information you'd like to provide about this individual. Click **OK** to add the entry to the Address Book.

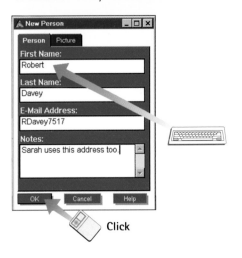

Click

4 Add More Addresses

In the **Address Book** window, note that your new entry is listed by your acquaintance's real name. (If your Address Book already included some names, they'll show up in this list, too.) To create additional addresses, repeat Steps 2 and 3.

5 Use the Address Book

Now you can use the Address Book to address a mail message. With the Address Book and a **Write Mail** window open, select the desired name from the Address Book and click **Send To**, **Copy To**, or **Blind Copy** to add that person's email address to the corresponding text box. To add multiple addresses to the message's **Send To** or **Copy To** text box, repeat this step as needed; the Address Book automatically separates multiple addresses with commas. When you're done adding addresses from your Address Book, click the window's close or Minimize button to get the Address Book out of your way. Complete and send the message as you would normally.

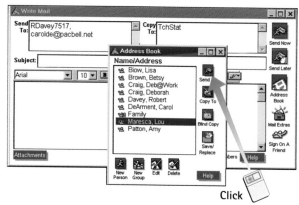

Click

End

How-To Hints

More About the Address Book

AOL 5.0 lets you transfer your Address Book from one computer to another. Click the **Save/Replace** button in the **Address Book** window. Then choose **Save the Address Book for your current screen name** and click **OK**; in the **Save Folder** dialog box, choose where to save your Address Book file. (If you're moving to a different computer, you can save the file to and retrieve it from a floppy disk.) To use this Address Book file on a different computer, go to that computer and open the Address Book there. Choose **Save/Replace** again, but this time select **Replace the Address Book for your current screen name** and choose the name of the Address Book file you saved.

You can store groups of email addresses under a single group name. For example, if you regularly converse with five friends about camping, you can group those friends' five email addresses under the single name **Camping**. To create an address group, open the Address Book and click the **New Group** button. Type a group name in the **Group Name** text box, type each group member's email address—separated by commas—in the **Addresses** text box, and then click **OK**.

How to Format Mail Messages

If you've been feeling that your email messages look too humdrum, you might like to know how to spiff them up a bit—by changing fonts, font sizes, font styles, and even text colors and background colors. In addition, AOL provides a number of different stationeries you can use if you get bored with plain white pages. (However, keep in mind that non-AOL users may not be able to see all your fancy formatting.) A word of warning here: You can have fun with these features, but don't go overboard or you might make things hard on your readers' eyes.

Begin

1 Select the Text to Modify

Click the **Write** toolbar button to open a **Write Mail** window. Enter the address and subject and begin typing the text of your message as usual. Select the text you want to modify; you can select anything from a single word to the entire message. (Dragging across text is a standard way to select it.)

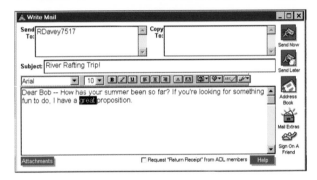

2 Change the Font Style

To change the selected text to a different font style, click the **B** (bold), **I** (italic), or **U** (underline) toolbar button in the **Write Mail** window. You can click more than one of these buttons to make a word both bold and italic, for example. (To turn off any of these features, just select the formatted text and click the button a second time.)

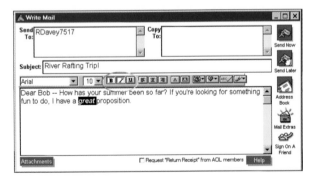

3 Change the Font and Font Size

To change the selected text to a different font, click the arrow next to the **Font** drop-down list and select the desired font. To choose a new font size, click the arrow next to the **Font Size** drop-down list and select the desired size.

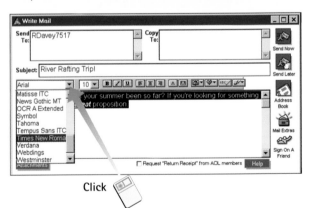

Click

4 Change the Text Alignment

To change the text alignment, click the **Align Left** (the default), **Center**, or **Align Right** button in the **Write Mail** window. In this case, you don't need to select any text if you're just aligning the current paragraph. If you want to align multiple paragraphs, first select the paragraphs. To reinstate the default alignment, click **Align Left**.

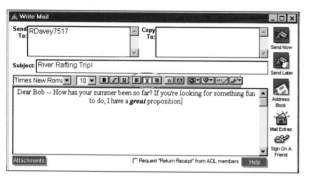

5 Change the Text Color

To change the color of your text, select the text to be modified and click the **Text Color** button (it looks like a blue letter **A** on a gray background). In the **Color** dialog box, choose a text color and click **OK**.

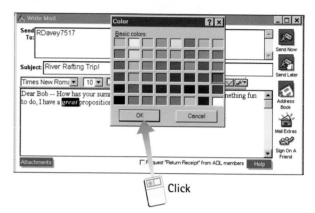

Click

6 Change the Background Color

To change the background color of your message, click the **Background Color** button (it looks like a gray letter **A** on a blue background). In the **Color** dialog box, choose a background color and click **OK**. Be careful to choose a background color that contrasts sufficiently with the text color; otherwise your text will be difficult if not impossible to read (for example, you won't be able to read blue text on a blue background).

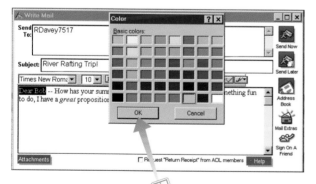

Click

End

How-To Hints

Making Changes Before You Type

You just learned how to type a message and then apply formatting changes to it. Often, you can also turn on the formatting and then begin to type your message. For example, if you want to write your entire message in the Times New Roman font, you could choose that font and then begin to type.

Choosing Stationery

AOL provides several different prefab stationeries you can choose from. Click the **Mail Extras** button in the **Write Mail** window. In the **Mail Extras** window, click **Stationery**. In the **Stationery** window that appears, select a stationery and click the **Preview** button to see what it looks like. If you decide to use the stationery, click the **Create** button, add your name (or initials) and screen name as requested, click **Create** again, and then type and send your message as usual in the **Write Message** window.

How to Create a Personalized Signature File

AOL 5 lets you create personalized *signature files*, which you can design to your specifications and then insert into your email messages. You can construct up to five signatures per screen name. For example, you can create several signature files, using one for correspondence with friends and family and another for work.

1 Choose Set up Mail Signatures

Click the **Mail Center** toolbar icon and choose **Set up Mail Signatures**. The **Set up Signatures** dialog box opens.

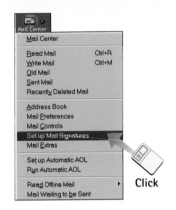

Click

2 Choose Create

Click the **Create** button. (If you've already set up a signature or two, you'll see them here.) The **Create Signature** dialog box opens.

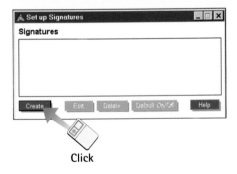

Click

3 Create Your Signature

In the **Signature Name** box, type a name for your signature (such as **Work** or **Friends**). Then type the signature itself. In addition to your name, you may want to include such information as your address and your phone or fax number. You can choose different font and font sizes, different text alignments, and different text and background colors—these formats all work as described in the preceding task.

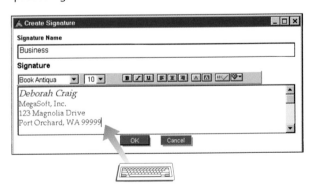

4 View Your Signature File

Click **OK** when you're done. You'll return to the **Set up Signatures** window, where you can see your newly created signature file. Repeat Steps 2 through 4 to create up to five signatures per screen name.

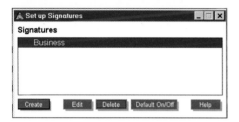

5 Insert a Signature

To insert your signature into an email message, create the email as usual. Whenever you want to insert the signature, click the **Insert Signature File** button (it's the one at the end of the toolbar in the **Write Mail** window) and choose your signature from the menu that appears.

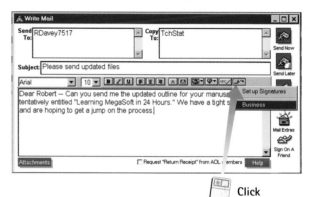

Click

6 Modifying Your Signature

AOL inserts the signature into your email message. At this point, you can edit your signature if you want. You might decide to change its position (maybe you want it at the top of the email message instead), its font attributes, or the content (you may decide to include your phone number). If you want to modify the signature's format or content for good rather than just in this particular email message, open the **Set Up Signatures** window, select the signature you want to modify, click **Edit**, make any needed changes, and click **OK**.

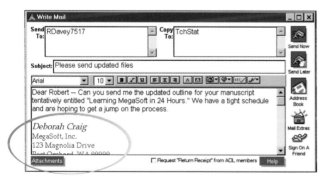

End

How-To Hints

Setting Up a Default Signature

You can set up a default signature, which is automatically inserted into every email you create. To do so, open the **Set up Signatures** dialog box (choose **Set up Mail Signatures** from the **Mail Center** menu). Select the signature you want to set as the default and click the **Default On/Off** button. A red check mark appears to the left of the signature. (To turn off the default, click the **Default On/Off** button again.) The next time you create an email message, the selected signature is inserted into it automatically.

Signatures Don't Work for Guests

Unfortunately, you can't use custom signatures when you're signed on as a guest user. (For details on signing on as a guest user, check out Task 3, "How to Retrieve Mail Remotely," earlier in this part.)

How to Check Your Spelling

Email is typically a fairly casual form of communication, in which a certain number of incomplete sentences, dubious grammatical constructions, and typos tend to be tolerated. But at times you may want to adhere to a higher standard, such as when you are sending out a particularly important email that you want to make sure is just right. In either case, you can benefit from using AOL's spell checker. In addition, you can further fine-tune your writing by using the thesaurus and dictionary.

Begin

1 Start the Spell Checker

Compose your email message normally and then position the insertion point at the beginning of the document. Click the **Spell Check** button on the **Formatting** toolbar. (If you don't start at the top of the document, AOL will at some point ask whether you want to start spell checking from the beginning of the document.)

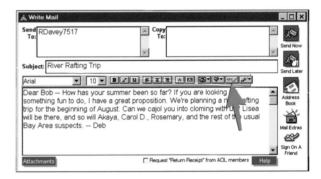

2 Choose a Suggested Word

If AOL finds a word it doesn't recognize, it stops on the word, displays the **Check Spelling** window, and may provide alternative spellings. If you see the correct spelling in the **Suggestions** list, click it to select it and then click **Replace** to insert the new word into your message. (If the same spelling error occurs repeatedly, you can correct all the misspellings at once by clicking **Replace All**.)

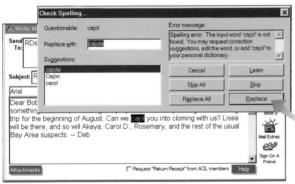

Click

3 Type the Correct Spelling

If the spell checker stops on a typo but AOL doesn't suggest any suitable alternative spellings, you can type the correct spelling in the **Replace with** text box and click the **Replace** button.

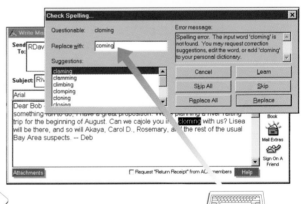

4 Skipping Words

If the spell checker stops on a word that you want to leave as is (many proper nouns and product names fall into this category), click the **Skip** button to move on without making any changes. (You can also click **Skip All** to skip all instances of this particular spelling.)

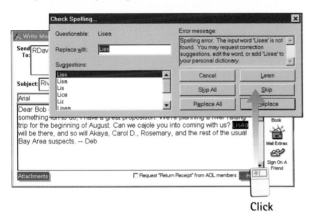

Click

5 Learning Words

If you want to add a word to the dictionary so that the spell checker never stops on it again, click the **Learn** button. (You would do this, for example, if you knew you'd be using this word again in future emails and didn't want the spell checker to stop on it again.)

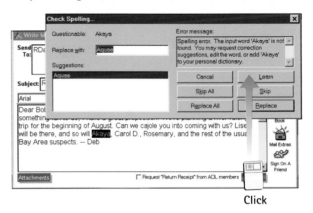

Click

6 Finish the Spell Check

After the spell checker has stopped on all words it doesn't recognize, it tells you that the spell check is complete. Click **OK**. Now you can send off your message as usual.

Click

End

How-To Hints

Customizing the Spell Checker

To customize how the spell checker operates, click the **My AOL** icon on the toolbar, choose **Preferences**, and click the **Spelling** icon in the Preferences window. In the **Spelling Preferences** window, check the boxes for the attributes you want to turn on.

Using the Thesaurus

AOL provides a thesaurus you can use to fine-tune your writing. Choose **Edit, Thesaurus** from the menu bar to open the **Thesaurus** window.

Using the Dictionary

To open the dictionary, choose **Edit, Dictionary** from the menu bar. Enter the word you want to look up in the top text box and click **Look Up**. AOL displays any matching entries in the lower text box. Double-click an entry to display its definition.

How to Use AOL Mail

AOL Mail is AOL's Web access to your mailbox. If you have a second ISP (Internet service provider) connection—one you access from work, for instance—you can check your AOL mailbox through Microsoft's Internet Explorer browser. First you must open an AOL Mail Web page. Then, each time you want to access your mailbox from the Web, you enter your screen name and password when prompted. Your AOL mailbox on the Web will be as easy to use as the one you use in your America Online for Windows software.

Begin

1 Go to the AOL Mail Page

Open your Microsoft Internet Explorer browser and enter the URL **http://www.aol.com/aolmail/**. Read the notes on the AOL Mail home page and then click **Read my AOL Mail now**.

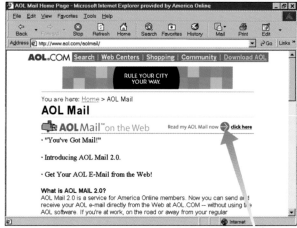

Click

2 Sign on to AOL Mail

You'll be prompted to sign on to AOL Mail. Enter your screen name and password in the designated text boxes and click **Enter AOL Mail**.

3 Decide Whether to Save Your Password

You may be asked whether you want to save your password. Click **No** to continue without saving your password. (You can choose **Yes** if you think it's both convenient and safe for you to do so.) Next you'll see a security alert; click **OK** to continue. (Feel free to select the check box if you don't want to see the warning in the future.)

Click

4 Complete the Sign-in to AOL Mail

You'll see a screen welcoming you to AOL Mail. Click the **Please click here to complete the sign-in process** button. You'll see a message warning you that you'll be leaving a secure Internet connection, allowing others to potentially view the mail you send. (You can choose not to see the warning in the future if you want.) Click **Yes** to continue. Your AOL mailbox appears.

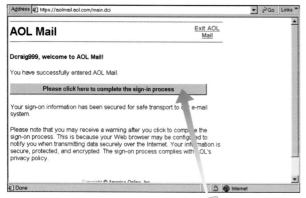

Click

5 Read Your AOL Mail

To read a message, click its subject line. The message opens in a window of its own, just as it does when you're actually running AOL.

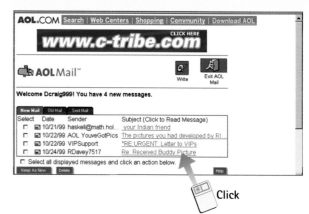

Click

6 Work with Your Mail

Use the buttons on the right side of the message window to reply to or forward the message. Use the buttons at the top (or bottom) to close the message (which returns you to the mailbox), delete the message, or save it as a new message (keeping it with your new incoming mail). You can also use the **Next** and **Prev** buttons to move through your mail messages.

How-To Hints

Viewing Old and Sent Mail

You can view your old mail and sent mail by clicking the **Old Mail** and **Sent Mail** tabs, just as you normally do.

Composing a New Message

To compose a new message, go to the mailbox window shown in Step 5 and click **Write**. An **AOL Mail** window appears. Address and write your message just as you do on AOL. (One difference and drawback is that you don't have access to your Address Book.) When you have completed your message, click **Send Now**.

Exiting AOL Mail

When you are finished reading and sending mail with AOL Mail, click the **Exit AOL Mail** button.

End

How to Set Up Buddy Lists

Buddy Lists help you keep track of the friends and family you like to interact with online. You create one or more lists of buddies from your family, school, work, and so on. AOL then notifies you when those members come online. After finding out who's online, you can locate your buddies and join them if they're in a chat area, send them Instant Messages, or invite an individual or group of friends to join you in a private chat room. When you know who is online, it's easy to get together and talk about your favorite topics or share an AOL keyword or Favorite Place.

1 Buddy List

Click the **My AOL** icon and select **Buddy List**. (You can also use the keyword **BUDDY**; refer to Part 1, Task 9, "How to Use Keywords," for more information on keywords.) The **Buddy List Setup** window opens.

Click

2 Choose a Buddy List Group

Note that AOL has already created three groups for you: **Buddies**, **Family**, and **Co-Workers**. Select any of these groups and click **Edit** to add names to that group. (You can also click **Create** if you want to add a brand new group). An **Edit List Buddies** window opens.

Click

3 Add Buddies to the Buddy List

Enter the screen name of the person you want to add to the list and click **Add Buddy**. Repeat this step to add as many buddies as you want. (Feel free to modify the buddy list group name while you're at it; just type the new name in the **Change Buddy List Group Name to** text box. Like screen names, Buddy List group names can be up to 16 characters and can include special characters such as **&** or **#**.) When you have finished adding screen names, click **Save**.

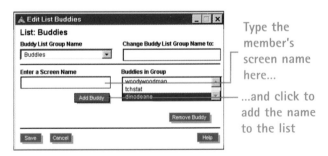

Type the member's screen name here...

...and click to add the name to the list

4 Confirm the Buddy List

A dialog box informs you that your list has been updated or created. Click **OK**.

Click

5 View a Buddy List

To view your buddy list and monitor who's online, open the **Buddy List Setup** window (choose **My AOL, Buddy List**) and select the list in question. Then click **View**. The **Buddies Online** window opens.

Click

6 Monitor Your Buddies Online

Whenever one of the screen names in your Buddy Lists is online, the screen name appears in the **Buddies Online** window below the list to which it belongs. This window is displayed by default each time you connect to AOL. (If you don't want this window to pop up automatically, click the **Buddy List Preferences** button in the **Buddy List Setup** window and deselect the **Show me my Buddy List(s) immediately after I sign on to AOL** check box.)

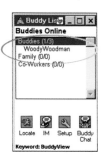

End

How-To Hints

Finding Your Buddies

You may have some buddies whose email addresses you're not sure of. If so, you can click the **Member Directory** button in the **Buddy List Setup** window (shown in Step 2) to search for them in AOL's Member Directory. You learned how to use this directory in Part 2, Task 13, "How to Find AOL Members."

Who's Online

By default, when you sign on, your **Buddies Online** window also opens, telling you which members in your lists are already online. If you leave this window open, each time a member of one of your Buddy Lists signs on, the window will be updated. An asterisk appears next to the screen name of the person who most recently signed on.

Redisplaying the Buddy List Window

If you've closed your **Buddy List** window and need to reopen it, click the **People** icon on the toolbar and select **View Buddy List**. Alternatively, choose the list in the **Buddy List Setup** window and click **View**.

How to Send Instant Messages

Instant Messages are a great way to get someone's attention—to invite him or her to join you in a chat room, ask a quick question, or just start a conversation. Each Instant Message is a private, person-to-person communication. Unlike email, Instant Messages are live interactions between two AOL members; you can only send these messages to someone who is already online. The only real delay is how long it takes to type your response and send it.

Begin

1 Open an Instant Message Window

To open an Instant Message window, click the **People** icon and choose **Instant Message**. (You can also press **Ctrl+I** to accomplish the same thing.) The **Send Instant Message** window opens.

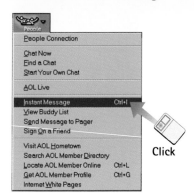

Click

2 Type the Screen Name

In the **To** box, type the screen name of the person to whom you're sending a message. To see whether your acquaintance is online before you send the message, click the **Available?** button.

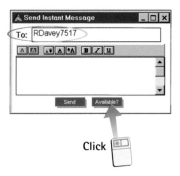

Click

3 Check Whether Person Is Online

A dialog box opens, informing you whether the person is online (you can't send Instant Messages to people who aren't online). Click **OK** to close this box.

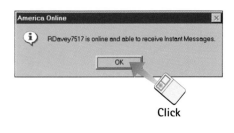

Click

4 Type and Send the Message

In the **Send Instant Message** dialog box, type your message in the text box and click **Send**.

Click

5 Respond to an Instant Message

Your acquaintance will receive the message in an **Instant Message** window that lists you as the sending party. There's a good chance he or she will write you back, in which case you'll see the message in the upper pane of an Instant Message window like this one. (You may also hear a tone to signal the incoming message.) To respond to an Instant Message, just type your response in the lower pane and click the **Send** button. If you do not want to respond to the message, click **Cancel**.

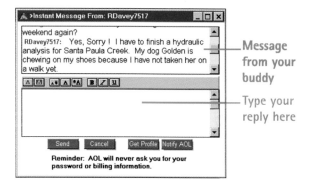

Message from your buddy

Type your reply here

6 Continue the Exchange

Continue exchanging messages with your acquaintance by entering your responses in the lower pane and clicking **Send**.

End

How-To Hints

Quick Instant Messages

If your **Buddy List** window is open (there's a good chance it will be open by default), you can send an Instant Message just by selecting the name of a buddy who's online and then clicking the **IM** button. (*IM* is online lingo for Instant Message.) Of course, this method only works for people you've designated as your buddies. Check the preceding task for details on how to do this.

Reviewing Instant Messages

If you want to review your Instant Message exchange, use the scrollbar in the upper pane of the Instant Message window.

How to Control Instant Messages

When you're exchanging Instant Messages, you might want to inform yourself about the person you're exchanging messages with, or (under more extreme circumstances) to inform AOL that you are receiving unwanted or inappropriate Instant Messages from someone. You can also turn off Instant Messages for your current AOL session if you want to ensure that you won't be interrupted or annoyed in any way.

Begin

1 Choose Get Profile

At any time during an Instant Message exchange, you can get the member profile of the person who's sending you messages. (You'll learn about creating member profiles in Part 4.) To do so, click the **Get Profile** button at the bottom of the **Instant Message** window.

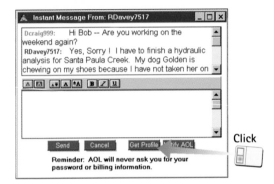

Click

2 Review the Sender's Member Profile

You'll see a **Member Profile** window similar to this one. Hopefully, the profile will give you some sense of whom you're conversing with—of course, it depends on how much information the user has provided about himself or herself. (Keep in mind that not all users fill out member profiles, and not all those who do are 100-percent forthcoming!) When you're done reviewing the profile, clear it from the screen by clicking the close button in the upper-right corner.

Click

3 Choose Notify AOL

Unfortunately, it's not out of the question for you to receive unsolicited or inappropriate Instant Messages. AOL now provides a way to contend with this problem. At the bottom of the Instant Message window, click the **Notify AOL** button.

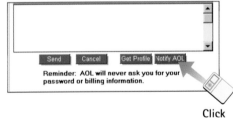

Click

4 Fill Out the Notify AOL Screen

You'll see a **Notify AOL** screen, in which you can comment on the nature of your complaint. The contents of the Instant Message are automatically included in your report. When you're done, click the **Send Report** button.

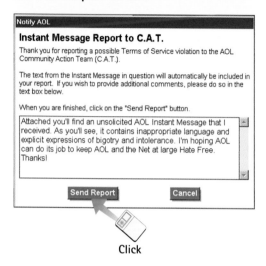

Click

5 Turn Off Instant Messages

If you prefer not to receive Instant Messages during your current AOL session, you can tell AOL to stop sending them during the current session. Press **Ctrl+I** to open an **Instant Message** window, then type **$im_off** in the **To** text box. In the message text field, type any character and click **Send**. A dialog box informs you that you are now "ignoring" Instant Messages.

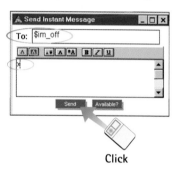

Click

6 Turn Instant Messages Back On

If you decide you want to receive Instant Messages again, send another Instant Message, but this time type **$im_on** in the **To** text box; again type any character in the message text field and click **Send**. A dialog box tells you that you are no longer ignoring Instant Messages.

Click

End

How-To Hints

Blocking Instant Messages

If you find Instant Messages an annoying intrusion rather than a pleasant break from your normal routine, you can block them altogether. Parents, in particular, may want to protect their children by ensuring that they don't receive unsolicited Instant Messages. Blocking Instant Messages is a simple process described in Part 6, Task 6, "How to Set Up Instant Message and Web Controls."

Instant Messages from AOL

Note that the America Online staff can send you Instant Messages even if you've turned them off.

How to Send Instant Messages over the Internet

Now you can send Instant Messages to friends and family who use other Internet service providers—provided that they register with AOL and install some special software called AOL Instant Messenger (go to **http://www.aol.com/aim/home.html**). After your friend has registered, he or she must download and install the AOL Instant Messenger software (AIM, for short). This is easy to do if your friend follows the onscreen instructions. This task describes how to use AOL Instant Messenger.

Begin

1 Sign On

After you (actually, *your friend*) install the AOL Instant Messenger software, start the software if necessary. (To start Instant Messenger, choose its desktop shortcut if you created one. Alternatively, open the **Start** menu and choose **Programs, AOL Instant Messenger, AOL Instant Messenger**.) In the dialog box that appears, click **Register new screen name.** Type your screen name (as registered with AOL) in the **Screen Name** box, type your password, and click **Sign On**.

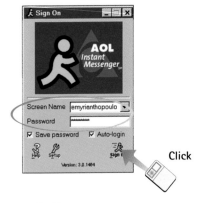

Click

2 Set Up Your Buddy List

A **Buddy List** window appears when your connection to AOL is complete. Use the **List Setup** tab to enter the screen names of your buddies (those you want to exchange Instant Messages with); return to the **Online** tab to see if someone is online. To send a message to a buddy who is online, select the buddy's name and click the **Send Instant Message** button (it looks like a single person with a speech bubble).

Click

3 Send an Instant Message

The **Instant Message** window opens. Type the text of your message and click **Send**.

Click

4 Accept the Instant Message

If you're an AOL user receiving an Instant Message from someone who's not an AOL member, you'll see a "knock knock" message, giving you the chance to accept or decline the message coming from the Internet. (You don't have this opportunity with Instant Messages from AOL members, although you can turn off Instant Messages altogether, as described in the previous task.) Click **OK** to receive the message.

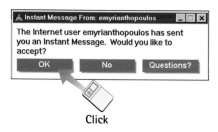

Click

5 View and Reply to Messages

If you accept the message, you'll see a window something like the one shown here. Use the lower text box to type a reply and click **Send**. Continue sending and receiving messages. If necessary, use the scrollbar to review a previous message.

6 Sign Off

When you are finished exchanging messages, choose **File, Close** from the **Buddy List** window. When asked whether you want to end this AOL Instant Messenger session, click **Yes**.

Click

End

How-To Hints

Getting Help

For help with AOL Instant Messenger software, choose **File, Help** from the menu bar in the **Buddy List** window.

If You're Away from Your Computer

If you'll be away from your computer, open the **Buddy List** window and choose **File, Away Message** to create a new away-from-my-desk message or to modify an old message. Anyone who tries to contact you will receive this message.

Adding and Deleting Buddies

To add a buddy in the **List Setup** tab, select a list and click the **Add A Buddy** button (it looks like a person with a plus sign). Then enter the buddy's screen name in the area provided and press **Enter**. To delete a buddy, select the screen name and click the **Delete Item** button (it looks like a person with a minus sign).

How to Read a Message Board

To prevent message board chaos, AOL provides dozens of subject-specific boards. This way, members interested primarily in politics, for instance, don't have to wade through dozens of messages on health. When you find a board that interests you, the first logical step is to read the board to see what kind of discussions and debates are there. This task shows you how to get to know a message board on your first visit.

Begin

1 Hunt for Message Boards

As you explore AOL, keep your eye out for items that lead to message boards—often they'll display pushpin icons or include the word *message* or *board*. For example, here's an item that leads to a list of *Star Trek* bulletin boards. (I got here by entering the keyword **Trek** and double-clicking **The Message Boards**.) If you'd like to explore some other message board instead, feel free to do so.

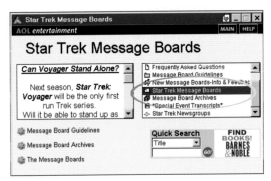

2 List the Message Boards

From this screen, double-click the **Star Trek Message Boards** item. You'll see a window listing the *Star Trek*-related message boards. Find a topic that interests you (scroll if necessary), click that topic, and then click **List All** (or double-click the topic). Alternatively, click **List Unread** to view only the postings to that board that you have not already read.

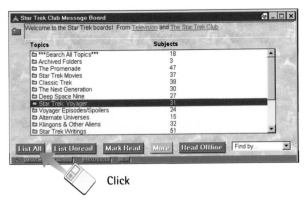

Click

3 List All Messages Under a Topic

A new window opens, listing available topics. Scroll to find a topic that interests you, click that topic, and then click **List All** (or double-click the topic).

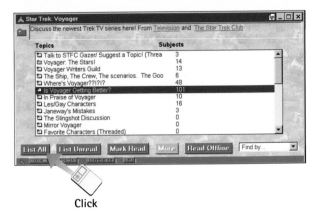

Click

4 Open a Message

A list of messages for the selected topic appears. Select any message in the list box and click **Read Post** (or double-click the message). The selected message opens in a new window.

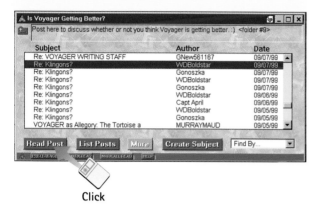

Click

5 Read a Message

If necessary, scroll to read the message. When you're done reading the current message, click **Next Post** to display the next message in the current *thread*—a message and a series of responses to it—or review earlier messages in the thread by clicking the **Previous Post** button. (If the message doesn't have any associated responses, or if the message board is not *threaded*, the **Next Post** and **Previous Post** buttons are grayed out.)

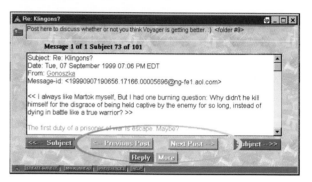

6 Read More Subjects

To read about a different subject in the current message board, click the << **Subject** or **Subject** >> button. These buttons dim when you come to the beginning or end of the list of messages.

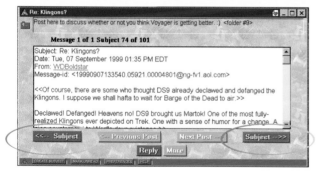

End

How-To Hints

Viewing Selected Messages

If there are too many messages for you to read in one session, use the **Find** drop-down list box. (This option appears in the lower-right corner of the **Message Board** window when you're viewing topics or subjects, but doesn't show up when you're looking at individual postings). This feature allows you to hunt for messages by date, or by a word or phrase contained in the message. (When you search by date, you can look at only new messages—that is, messages posted since you last visited this board. You can also look for messages that have been posted in the last *x* number of days, or between two dates that you specify.) The **Custom Search** option lets you search using both dates and search phrases.

How to Post a Message to a Message Board

Just reading a message board is akin to listening in on a conversation but never contributing what you think. To take an active part in conversation, you must post your own messages. At the same time, remember that your message may be read by many people from varying backgrounds, so be careful what you write and how you write it. In general, avoid profanity, snide and discriminatory remarks, and personal attacks.

Begin

1 Reply to a Message

Find and open the bulletin board message you want to respond to and then click the **Reply** button. (If you're not sure how to find the message, refer to the previous task, "How to Read a Message Board.") The **Reply** window opens.

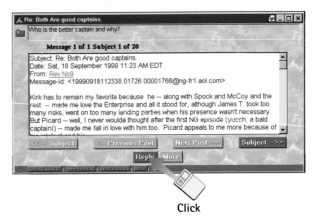

Click

2 The Author and Subject Lines

Notice that the **Author** and **Subject** lines in the **Reply** window are already filled with information taken from the original posting, and the **Post to message board** check box is selected by default. In addition, the text of the original message is displayed in the pane on the left.

3 Type and Send Your Reply

Type your reply in the **Reply** window and then click the **Send** button. When you receive the confirmation that your message has been sent, simply click **OK** to proceed. Although you have virtually unlimited space when typing a message, keep in mind that few readers have the interest or inclination to read long messages.

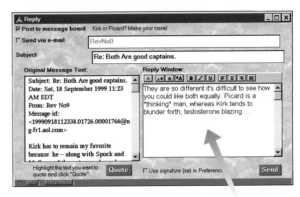

4 Creating a New Subject

To add a new topic instead of replying to an existing message, click the **Create Subject** button. (A message and all the responses to it are known as a *thread*.) Of course, the subject should still be relevant to the topic folder you're in. (Don't insert a message on backyard composting in a message board on *Star Trek Voyager*!)

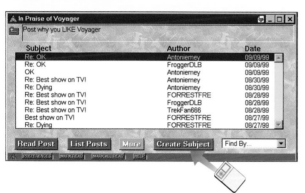

Click

6 Send the Message

Type your subject line and message and click the **Send** button to post the message. As before, you'll get a confirmation dialog box that your message has been sent; click **OK**.

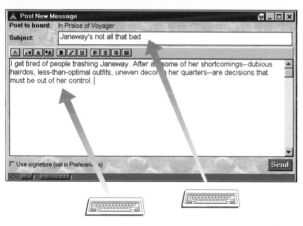

End

5 Enter the New Message

Notice that the top of the **Post New Message** window lists the topic area to which the new message will be posted; in this case, **In Praise of Voyager**.

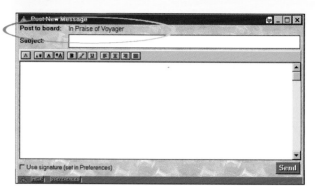

How-To Hints

Replying with Email

You can respond directly to the author of a message by selecting the **Send via e-mail** check box in the **Reply** window. Your message goes directly to the author and is not posted to the bulletin board.

Setting Up a Signature

If you want to lend a personal touch to your postings, you can create a signature. Just click the **Preferences** button at the bottom of the message board window, click the **Posting** tab, and type in the **Signature** text box. You can enter anything you like—your name and address, a favorite quote, or whatever else suits your fancy (it's better to be short and sweet rather than long winded). When posting your messages, make sure to check the **Use signature** check box.

Task

PART 4

Chatting

*C*hatting is the electronic equivalent of a face-to-face or telephone conversation; there's virtually no time lag between sending a message and receiving a response. The **People Connection** area is AOL's place to discuss a wide variety of topics in small groups and to meet with guests in large groups. As you'll discover, you can have some absolutely fascinating—and some rather bottom-of-the-barrel—exchanges in chat rooms. Read on to find out how it all works. ●

How to Chat

AOL has dozens of different chat rooms. Even though most of them focus on a specific subject, no matter what chat room you visit, the techniques for chatting are similar. If you're new to chatting, an interesting chat room to visit is the **Lobby**, a chat room without any specific focus. Like a hotel lobby, AOL's **Lobby** is usually full of people going from one place to another, and a few are usually willing to linger a while and have a conversation. This task shows you how to visit the **Lobby** and how to chat. Note that the **Lobby** is only one of AOL's many chat rooms; you'll learn about visiting other chat rooms later in this part.

Begin

1 Choose Chat Now

Make sure that you're signed on to AOL. Click the **People** icon and choose **Chat Now**. A **Lobby** window opens.

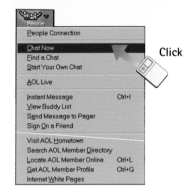

Click

2 Enter the Lobby

The automated OnlineHost greets you by telling you what **Lobby** you are in. If the original **Lobby** is full (chat rooms allow only 25 members at a time), you may find yourself in an alternative **Lobby**, such as **Lobby 1**, **Lobby 2**, and so on. Every **Lobby** works the same. (You can't visit a chat room that's already filled to its capacity—at least, not until someone leaves.)

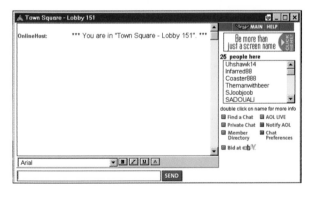

3 Type a Greeting

In the long text box at the bottom of the **Lobby** window, type a greeting message and click **Send**. (As with messages on message boards and email, it's better to avoid using all uppercase letters—the electronic equivalent of SHOUTING.)

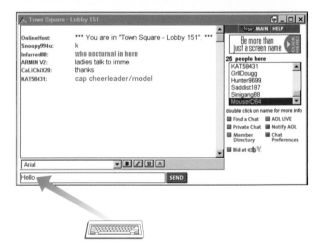

4 Read the Conversation

Your screen name appears in the window's central text box, followed by the message you just typed. Within seconds, someone else's message will appear in the text box. They may be responding to you, sending out a general greeting, or talking to someone else. Keep in mind that you've just entered a room full of people who may already be involved in other conversations. Also note that there's a lot of lingo here; you'll start to pick up on it after a while (see the How-To Hints for some suggestions on decoding this secret code).

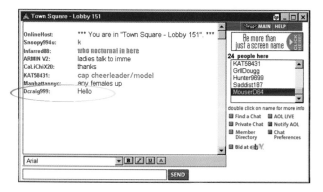

5 Answer Back

When someone responds to you, respond in turn by typing a message in the long text box and clicking **Send**. To indicate to whom you're responding (out of the possible 25 room occupants), you may want to include that member's screen name—or some abbreviation of it—in your response. (Uppercase is acceptable when it's part of someone's screen name.)

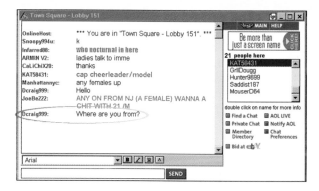

6 Say Goodbye

Continue to receive and send messages as desired. When you're done chatting, you might want to send out a goodbye message. Wait a few moments for other members' goodbye responses, and then close the **Lobby** window.

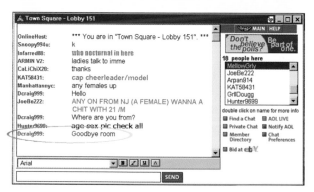

End

How-To Hints

Contending with Junk Mail

Be forewarned that when you begin visiting chat rooms, you may start to receive a lot of unsolicited junk mail, much of it of a very dubious nature. Check Task 7, "How to Navigate People Connection," later in this part, for some hints on how to avoid being besieged by such email.

Online Shorthand

You may find that some chat messages include online shorthand such as **:)** and **LOL**. To learn more about online shorthand, choose **Help, Member Services Online Help** from the menu bar. In the **Member Services** window, select **People Connection**. Make sure that the **Chatting Online** tab is selected and choose **Understanding Symbols & Shorthand**.

How to Create a Member Profile

If you're starting an online conversation, it can take a lot of time to ask a person about his or her real name, hobbies, occupation, and so on. Enter *member profiles*: online personal-information forms that many members fill out for other members to use. If your online chat partner has filled out a member profile, you can look at that profile to gain some insight into him or her. This task explains how you can create a member profile of your own, which other members can access.

Begin

1 Choose My Member Profile

Make sure that you're signed on to AOL. Click the **My AOL** icon in the toolbar and choose **My Member Profile**.

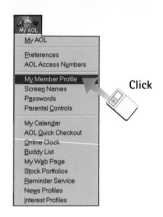

Click

2 Read the Warning

You may see a warning, reminding you that information you enter in your profile is public—*very* public. AOL has millions of members, and all of them can look at your member profile. Click **OK** to acknowledge the warning and continue. (If you don't want to see the warning again, select the **Please do not show me this again** check box.)

> **Remember: Your AOL Member Profile is available to the entire AOL community.**
>
> Member Profiles in the AOL Member Directory can be seen by all AOL members. Do not post information you may want to keep private, such as your full name, address, telephone number or age. For more online safety tips, go to Keyword: Neighborhood Watch.
>
> ☐ Please do not show me this again
>
> OK

Click

3 Enter Your Profile

The **Edit Your Online Profile** window opens, offering several text boxes and option buttons you can use to describe yourself. You're not required to share personal information, so complete only those parts of your profile that you care to provide and then click **Update**.

Edit Your Online Profile			
To edit your profile, modify the category you would like to change and select "Update." To continue without making any changes to your profile, select			
Your Name:	Deborah Craig		
City, State, Country:	Oakland, CA		
Birthday:			
Sex:	○ Male	⊙ Female	○ No Response
Marital Status:			
Hobbies:	running, photography, music		
Computers Used:	Micron 333 Mhz		
Occupation:	Technical writer, musician, photographer		
Personal Quote:	"Failure is impossible," Susan B. Anthony		

Update   Delete   Cancel   My AOL   Help & Info

Click

4 Close the Confirmation Dialog Box

A dialog box informs you that your profile is being created. Click **OK** to close this dialog box.

Click

5 Get a Profile

To look at another person's profile, open the **Lobby** window and start a conversation with someone. To learn more about your chat partner, find and double-click that person's screen name in the list box in the **Lobby** window's upper-right corner. A window bearing his or her screen name opens. Click **Get Profile**.

Double-click

6 Read the Profile

If the person has filled out a member profile, that profile displays in a **Member Profile** window. (If the person hasn't filled out a member profile, a dialog box informs you that no profile is available.) Read the profile and return to the **Lobby**. Now you can talk about some of the things you have in common. It's a great way to start cementing your new friendship.

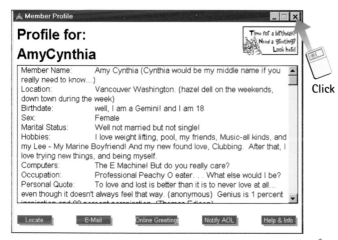

Click

End

How-To Hints

Use Caution with Your Profile

Information that you share in your personal profile is available to everyone on AOL—that's millions of people! Please be careful to share only information that is appropriate for everyone on AOL to know. **Parents:** Each screen name you create for your children can also have a member profile. Please discuss with your children the information they should enter in this window.

Other Ways to Look Up Profiles

Remember that you can look up the profiles of people who send you Instant Messages, as described in the Part 3, "Communicating." In addition, you can look up a member's profile by clicking the **People** icon and choosing **Get AOL Member Profile** from the **People Connection** menu. You'll be asked to enter the screen name of the person whose profile you want to find. This way you can track down profiles for people who aren't necessarily online.

How to Use Chat Features

The **People Connection** area offers more than just the opportunity to chat in small groups in chat rooms. AOL chat helps you meet people, find out information about them (with member profiles), and even send them Instant Messages—all without leaving your chat room. Because sometimes people rub you the wrong way, you even have the option to ignore people you just don't want in your conversation. AOL's wealth of features allow you to personalize your AOL chat sessions.

Begin

1 Enter a Chat Room

Make sure that you're signed on to AOL. Click the **People** icon in the toolbar and choose **Chat Now**. A **Lobby** window opens.

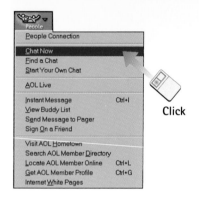

Click

2 Start Chatting

Begin participating in the chat room as you normally would (refer to Task 1, "How to Chat," if you're not sure what to do).

3 Pick a Person

As you watch and participate in the chat session, one person may stand out as someone you'd like to know more about or you'd like to be able to ignore. Locate the person's screen name in the **People Here** list box and double-click that name.

Double-click

4 Get a Profile or Send a Message

A screen name window opens for the selected person. If this is a person you want to know more about, click **Get Profile** as you did in the previous task. If this is a person you'd like to send a person-to-person message to, click **Send Message**. To experiment, click **Send Message** now.

Click

5 Send an Instant Message

A **Send Instant Message** window opens with the addressee's screen name already entered in the **To** text box. Enter your message in the message box and click **Send** to begin a private person-to-person conversation. (You learned about Instant Messages in Part 3.)

6 Ignore a Member

If you are in a room where another member's comments make you uncomfortable, select **Ignore Member** in the screen name dialog box. To return to your chat room, click the dialog box's close button. You will no longer see messages from the ignored screen name.

Click

End

How-To Hints

Handling Inappropriate Messages

If you find that a member's messages are inappropriate, click the **Notify AOL** button in the lower-right corner of the chat room window. Much like the **Notify AOL** button available in Instant Message windows, this feature allows you to notify AOL if you feel inappropriate comments are being made. Be forewarned that you'll feel the urge to do this often in some chat rooms!

More Chat Features

From any chat room window, you can gain access to a number of other chat features, including finding chat rooms of interest to you, setting up private chat sessions, setting up your chat preferences, and more. You'll learn about these features in the upcoming tasks.

How to Find Other Chat Rooms

When you used the chat features in the previous tasks, you may have noticed the **Find a Chat** button in the lower-right corner of the chat window. This button leads to a feature that enables you to track down just about any other chat room. The rooms you've been to so far are not topic specific, as you'll see in this task; however, you can use the **Find a Chat** feature to find chat rooms on subjects ranging from auto mechanics to astronomy.

Begin

1 Choose Find a Chat

Make sure that you're signed on to AOL. Click the **People** icon in the toolbar and choose **Find a Chat**. (If you're already in a chat room, you can click the **Find a Chat** button in the window's lower-right corner.) The **Find a Chat** window opens.

Click

2 Choose a Chat Room Category

Featured chats are indexed by category. Select a category in the list box on the left and click the **View Chats** button to see the chat rooms in that category in the list box on the right.

Click

3 Select a Chat Room

Select the chat room you want to enter from the list box on the right and click **Go Chat**. Regardless of what type of room you enter, the automated OnlineHost indicates what room you are in. Now you can participate in the discussion, as you learned how to do in the previous tasks. Remember, if your new room has a specific focus, you should try to stick to the topic at hand.

4 Visit Member Chats

AOL provides chat rooms created by People Connection; there are also chat rooms created by members. To get to these chat rooms, return to the **Find a Chat** window and click the **created by AOL Members** tab. Like the People Connection rooms, the member rooms are indexed by category. As you did before, select a category in the left list box, click **View Chats**, select a room on the right, and click **Go Chat** to visit the room.

Click

6 Move to Another Room

When you want to move from your room to another room, click the **Find a Chat** button. From the **Find a Chat** window, you can move to other chat rooms using the procedure described in Steps 2 and 3 of this task.

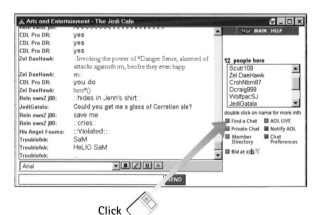

Click

 End

5 Begin to Chat

The member-created chat rooms are really no different than the People Connection rooms—although some of the subjects may be more offbeat. Again, remember to stick to the topic of the room.

How-To Hints

Categories of Chat Rooms

AOL's chat rooms fall into three categories: public rooms (permanent rooms that AOL has set up to address a variety of member interests); member rooms (rooms that members create to discuss a topic not addressed by an existing public room); and private rooms (temporary rooms that members create to discuss topics privately).

Other Features in the Chat Window

Notice that you can use the buttons in the chat window to create your own room (**Private Chat**), search the **Member Directory** (check Part 2, Task 13, "How to Find AOL Members," for the scoop on using the **Member Directory**), and set your chat preferences (covered in the next task), among other things.

How to Customize Chat

Chatting is a popular AOL feature. Just because so many members like to chat, however, doesn't mean they all agree on how the chat rooms should be set up. For this reason, AOL enables you to set up your own chat environment with **Chat Preferences**. You can customize the look of your session without affecting other members. You can monitor members leaving and entering the chat room you're in or allow the messages to appear double-spaced so that they're easier to read. Read on to find out more about customizing your chat sessions.

Begin

1 Choose Preferences

Make sure that you're signed on to AOL. Click the **My AOL** icon in the toolbar and choose **Preferences**. The **Preferences** window opens.

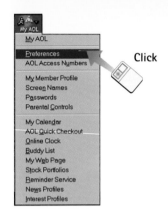

Click

2 Choose Chat

Click **Chat**. The **Chat Preferences** window opens. (You can also open the **Chat Preferences** window by clicking the **Chat Preferences** button in the lower-right corner of any chat room window.)

Click

3 View Chat Preferences

Preferences that are currently enabled have a check mark to their left. AOL automatically enables chat room sounds. By default, the other options—**Notify me when members arrive/leave, Double-space incoming messages**, and **Alphabetize the member list**—are turned off.

4 Put Your Preferences into Effect

Select the preferences you want to enable (or disable). If you're the cautious type, you may want to try one or two new features at a time to decide how well they work for you. When you've finished making your selections, click **OK**.

Click

5 Close the Confirmation Dialog

If you selected **Alphabetize the member list**, a dialog box informs you that your new list-order preferences will take effect when you begin a new chat session. Click **OK** to close the dialog box.

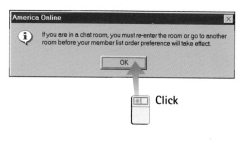

Click

6 Viewing Your New Preferences

Depending on the selections you made in Step 4, your window may look different from the one you see here. In this chat session, the lines are double-spaced, you're notified when members leave and enter the chat, and entries in the **People Here** box are in alphabetical order.

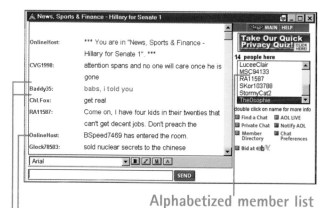

Alphabetized member list

Notification of entering members

Double-spaced messages

How-To Hints

Being Notified When Members Arrive or Leave

Turning on the **Notify me when members arrive and/or leave** items results in a printed message in your chat window each time a person enters or leaves the chat room you are visiting.

Playing Sounds in Chat Rooms

The **Enable chat room sounds** preference lets you hear when someone uses a sound file. For more information on using sound files in chat, select **Member Services Online Help** from the Help menu. Then click **People Connection** in the **Member Services** window and select **Playing Sounds in a Chat Room**.

End

How to Create Your Own Chat Room

If you can't find a chat room to suit you, you may want to create your own. There are several ways of going about this. In particular, you can create a member room, which is open to all other AOL members and is relatively easy for them to find. Or you can create a private chat room and invite just your friends or co-workers; for someone to get into this type of chat room, that person has to know its exact name.

Begin

1 Choose Start Your Own Chat

Make sure that you're signed on to AOL. Click the **People** icon in the toolbar and choose **Start Your Own Chat**. (You can also click **Start Your Own Chat** in the **Find a Chat** window.) The **Start Your Own Chat** window opens.

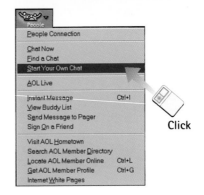

Click

2 Choose Member Chat or Private Chat

From this window, you can start either a **Member Chat** or a **Private Chat**. Member chats are listed in the **Created by AOL Members** tab in the **Find a Chat** window; any other interested AOL members can easily join in on them. Private chats are not listed; AOL members must know the exact name of the chat to be able to participate. You may want to set up a private chat with a bunch of your friends or a group of remote co-workers who want to have an

3 Create a Member Chat

online meeting.

If you click **Member Chat**, you'll see a window like this one. Double-click the name of the category under which you want your chat room to be listed. Then type a name for your room and click **Go Chat**.

Double-click

4 Enter the Chat Room

You'll be in your chat room. Because it's a brand-new room, you may find yourself all alone at first. You might want to encourage your friends to hop in and join you. If your friends are online already, you can send them an Instant Message to encourage them to jump in on the chat. If they're not online, you might have to break down and call them. You can even use email or phone mail to plan to meet in a certain chat at a designated time.

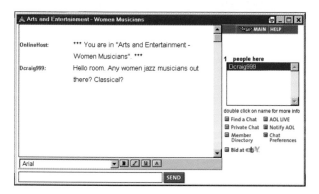

5 Find Your Chat Room

To check that chat room was created and is now listed, click **Find a Chat** in the lower-right corner of your chat window. In the **Find a Chat** window, click the **created by AOL Members** tab, select the category under which you decided to create your chat room, and scroll through the list of chat rooms on the right. Your new chat room should be listed.

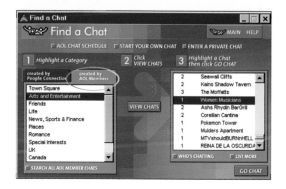

6 Create a Private Chat

To create a private chat, return to the **Start Your Own Chat** window (see Step 2) and click the **Private Chat** button. In the **Private Chat** window that opens, type the name of your chat and click **Go Chat**. Remember that nobody will be able to join you in this chat room unless you tell them its exact name.

End

How-To Hints

Entering a Private Chat Room

If someone gives you the name of a private chat room they want you to enter, simply choose **Enter a Private Chat** from the **Find a Chat** window (or click **Private Chat** from any chat room window), type the name of the private chat room you want to enter, and click **Go Chat**.

Disappearing Chat Rooms

Member-created chat rooms exist only as long as there is at least one person in the room. When the last person leaves the room, the room disappears and must be re-created before it can be used again. Chat rooms created by People Connection are always available, even if no one is in them.

How to Navigate People Connection

People Connection is like a one-stop shopping center for chat features. From here, you can tap into some familiar features such as the **Find a Chat** window. In addition, you can check out the **AOL Chat Schedule**, find out which are the "hot" chats of the moment, get a tour of chat features, learn about how to avoid junk mail, and more.

Begin

1 Choose People Connection

Make sure that you're signed on to AOL. Click the **People** icon in the toolbar and choose **People Connection**. The **Welcome to People Connection** window opens.

Click

2 Welcome to People Connection

From this window, you can gain access to a number of features you've already learned about, such as **Find a Chat** and **Chat Now!**.

3 Consult AOL's Chat Schedule

You can also take a look at the **AOL Chat Schedule**. Click **AOL Chat Schedule** under the **Chat** heading. From the **AOL Chat Schedule** window, you can look at what chats are going on at particular times or on particular days of the week. If you want to return to the **People Connection** window, click **Main**.

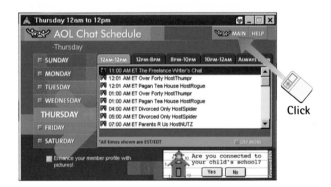

Click

4 Avoid Junk Mail

Receiving junk mail can be a huge problem on AOL, especially after you start visiting a chat room or two. For some helpful hints on how to avoid a deluge of (possibly offensive) junk mail, click **Avoid Junk Mail** under the **QuickStart** heading on the **Welcome to People Connection** window. You'll see a screen of detailed information on how to contend with the perennial problem of junk email.

5 Quick Steps to Chatting

If you're still relatively new to chatting and feel that you don't quite have your sea legs, try clicking **New to Chat?** under the **QuickStart** heading on the **Welcome to People Connection** window. The **New Members** window provides information on how to avoid *spam* (junk mail), how to learn some of the occasionally befuddling lingo associated with chatting, and much more. This screen also provides links to important topics such as **Chat Preferences** (you learned about these earlier), **Chat Etiquette**, and **Parental Controls**. (You'll find out more about supervising your children's online experience in Part 6, "Sharing America Online with Your Family.")

6 Check Out the "Hot" Chats

Click the **Today's Hottest Chats** link on the upper-right corner of the **Welcome to People Connection** window. In the **Today's Hottest Chats** window, scroll through the list box on the left to see whether any of the chats interest you. If you find one that stands out, click it to go there.

End

Task

Exploring the Internet

*T*he Internet (sometimes called *the Net*) is the world's largest network of computers. (A *network* of computers is simply a series of computers linked together so that they can communicate and share resources.) The Internet includes connections to research facilities, educational institutions, businesses, and online services worldwide. Through these connections, millions of people currently enjoy Internet access.

The tasks in this part introduce you to many of the Internet's features: newsgroups, mailing lists, FTP, and the wildly popular and successful World Wide Web (*the Web* for short). Although some people confuse the Web and the Net, the Web is actually a user-friendly subset of the Net that lets you click text and graphical links to travel easily from place to place. ●

How to Browse the World Wide Web

The World Wide Web (WWW) is a vast resource of business, personal, government, educational, and entertainment information. Web information appears in many different forms, including text, graphics, video, and even sound—all easily accessible with the use of a *browser*. Web browsers are user-friendly tools that enable you to navigate the Internet just by clicking with your mouse. In this task, you learn the basics of browsing so that you can go exploring on your own.

Begin

1 Choose Go to the Web

Make sure that you're signed on to AOL. Click the **Internet** icon on the toolbar and choose **Go to the Web**. (You can also click **Go to Web** in the lower-right corner of the **Welcome** window, if it's displayed.)

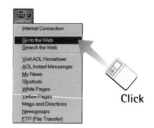

Click

2 Explore the Web Browser

The AOL.com Web home page opens. You're now in the Web browser. The AOL toolbar's **Previous**, **Next**, **Refresh**, and **Stop** buttons and the **Go** text box are especially useful when navigating the Web. Use the scrollbar to view more of a page.

3 Travel Using Links

Web pages are *hypertext documents*, which means that clicking a *link* takes you to another page. Links connect Web pages so that you can navigate quickly through huge volumes of information. Links can be text or images: Text links (sometimes called *hypertext links*) appear underlined and in color (typically blue). Image links are graphics. When you point to either type of link with your mouse, the link's URL appears at the bottom of the screen, and your mouse pointer typically changes into a hand.

4 Click More Links

When you click a link, a new page appears. You'll notice that the AOL icon in the upper-right corner of the screen pulsates as the page is loaded, indicating that the browser is working. (If you decide not to load the page, click the **Stop** button—it's the circle with the × in it on the toolbar.) Click another interesting link.

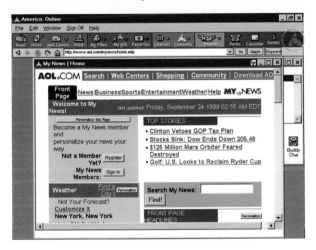

6 Go Forward a Page

When you click the **Previous** arrow, the page you viewed previously appears. Also note that the **Next** (right) arrow is now available; click the **Next** arrow to return to the page you saw in Step 5.

Click

5 Go Back a Page

Another new page appears for you to read and follow; click the links that interest you. To return to the page you were just on, click the **Previous** (left) arrow. You can click the **Previous** arrow repeatedly if you like.

Click

How-To Hints

Traveling to Internet Sites

Many AOL areas include links to Internet sites. Clicking an item designated as an Internet site brings up a Web browser window and loads the appropriate page.

Entering URLs

You'll often find references to Web sites listed as *URLs* (*uniform resource locators*). URLs provide the information on where to find the next page. All Web URLs begin with the characters **http:**, as in **http://mcp.com/**. To access these Web sites, sign on to AOL, type the URL in the **Go** text box, and press **Enter**. Make sure that you type the URL exactly as it is given to you. The great thing about URLs is that they enable you to go directly to a site without clicking a link.

Use the Correct Slash in URLs

Remember that URLs use the forward slash (/), not the backslash (\), which you might be used to from typing directory names in DOS or Windows.

End

How to Set Up WWW Preferences

You can customize your Web experience by setting your WWW preferences. You can turn off multimedia features to display pages more quickly; or you can change the colors of the text, background, and links. WWW preferences also enable you to choose which page you'd like to have loaded automatically when you open the Web browser. You'll learn the basics in this task and then you can make more changes on your own.

Begin

1 Choose Preferences

You don't have to be signed on to AOL to perform this task. Click the **My AOL** icon and select **Preferences**. The **Preferences** window opens.

Click

2 Click WWW

Click the **WWW** icon. The **AOL Internet Properties** dialog box opens.

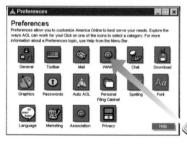

Click

3 Set Your General Preferences

Each tab in this dialog box has several features you can customize (you'll probably want to leave most of the these settings as AOL has set them). On the **General** tab shown here, you can change the address of your *home page* (the page that opens when you first start the browser), and adjust how long to keep track of the links you've visited. (When links are stored in the history folder, you can quickly revisit Web sites you've been to recently.)

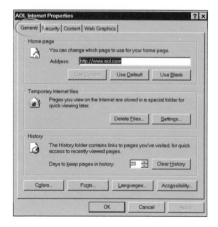

4 Finish Filling Out the Template

Scroll down and finish filling out the Web page template. In this example, enter a title, divider style, and some personal information about yourself such as what you look like, where you live, and what some of your hobbies are. You can also provide the links for some of your favorite online locations. For example, if you are fascinated with astronomy and space travel, you can provide the URL for NASA. (In case you're interested, it's **www.nasa.gov**.)

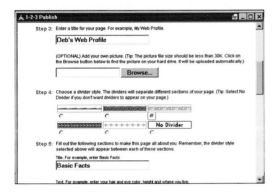

5 Preview Your Web Page

After you fill out the template, you can preview your Web page by clicking the **Preview My Page** button. A new window opens to display a preview of your Web page.

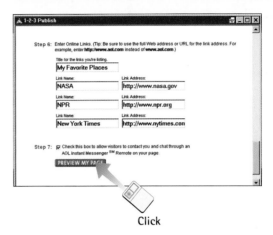

Click

6 Save Your Web Page

From the preview page, you can click **Save** to save your page or click **Modify** to tweak the page until it suits you. When you click **Save**, your Web page is saved and added to the **AOL Hometown** area automatically.

Click

End

How-To Hints

Sending Friends to Your Web Page

After you save your Web page, you'll see a screen confirming that it has been saved and listing the URL. (You'll also receive a congratulatory email message that lists the URL.) If you want friends to be able to see your newly created work of art, just give them the URL so that they can check it out for themselves.

Creating Pages with HotDog Express

1-2-3 Publish is simple to use, but it does have one big drawback: Pages you create with this program can't be edited with any other Web publishing tools. If you want to create a more sophisticated Web page that you have more control over, try experimenting with HotDog Express. Just click the **HotDog Express** link that appears in the initial **AOL Hometown** window to download the program.

How to Add Web Links to Email

In Part 3, "Communicating," you learned the basics of sending and receiving email. Now you can go beyond the basics of mail on AOL and send HTML mail or mail with live, clickable links. When you want to share a great Web page with your friends (such as the one you just created), you can add a link to your email message. All your friends need to do is click the link in your message. AOL's browser will open a window and connect to your link immediately.

Begin

1 Click Write

Make sure that you're signed on to AOL and then click the **Write** icon in the toolbar. A **Write Mail** window opens.

Click

2 Select the Link Text

Type the appropriate information in the **To** and **Subject** text boxes, then type your message in the message text box. Use your mouse to select the text for the **URL** link. (You can include the URL itself, or just some text saying something like **click here**.)

3 Choose Create Hyperlink

Right-click the selected text and choose **Insert a Hyperlink** from the context menu that appears. You'll see an **Edit Hyperlink** dialog box.

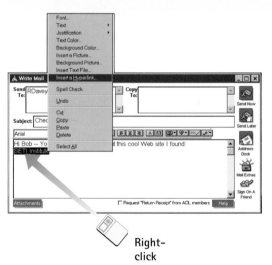

Right-click

4 Type the URL

Type the URL in the **Internet address** text box and click **OK**. Make sure that you type the URL exactly as it appeared in the status bar when you visited the page. Pay attention to spaces, slashes, tildes (~), and so on.

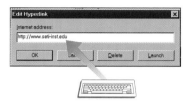

5 Send Your Message

The text you selected now appears highlighted and underlined. Finish typing your message and click **Send Now** to mail the message.

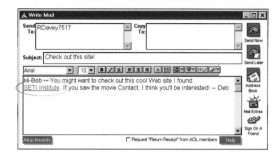

6 Following a Link

When you open a message that has a hyperlink included, the link is highlighted and underlined as you've seen in other Web pages. Click the highlighted text. (When you point to the link, you may see a tip box that lists the URL.) AOL opens a browser window and connects you directly to the URL indicated by the hyperlink.

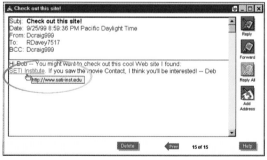

End

How-To Hints

Using Automatic AOL

If you're using Automatic AOL to get your mail, you must first sign on to AOL before you can make the hyperlink connection.

Your Email Program Must Be Browser Aware

Hypertext links appear in only those messages sent to other AOL members and Internet users with browser-aware email programs.

Another Way to Add Links

You can also add links to your email messages by beginning to compose your message, opening the Web site or AOL area you want to create a link to, and dragging the Favorite Places icon (the little heart) into the desired spot in the email message. This approach works well if you don't know the site's URL ahead of time.

How to Find People Using the White Pages

Are you trying to track down an old school friend, college roommate, or acquaintance you fell out of touch with? Use AOL NetFind's **Find a Person** feature—it's an online White Pages right at your fingertips. You can find a person's address and phone number just as you can in a regular phone book listing; if that person is registered, you can also find his or her email and Web address information. AOL has access to thousands of publicly available White Pages listings for the United States.

Begin

1 Choose White Pages

Make sure that you're signed on to **AOL**. Click the **Internet** toolbar icon and choose **White Pages**. The **AOL White Pages** window opens.

Click

2 Fill in the Information

Use the text boxes on this page to enter any information you have about the person you're trying to find (you don't need to fill in all the text boxes). Note that you must spell out city names; you cannot use any abbreviations.

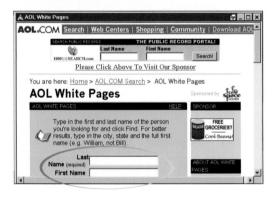

3 Click Find!

After you've filled in the text boxes with known information, click the **Find!** button. The **AOL White Pages Search Results** page appears.

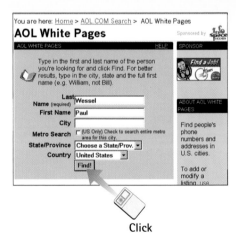

Click

4 View the Results

The results page displays all the listings that match your search query. As you can see, this window lets you know how many total matches were turned up.

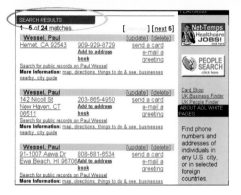

5 Find the Person

Scroll through the list box to find the person you're looking for. If necessary, click **Next 5** to move forward through the list of names; click **Previous 5** to move backward through the list.

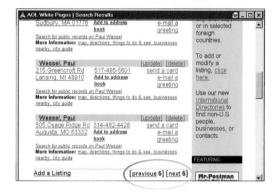

6 Send an Email

After you find the person you're looking for, you can send him or her an email by clicking **e-mail a greeting** (this link appears next to each entry in the results list). You'll land on a **PageGreetings** page, from which you can choose a category of greeting and a specific greeting to send electronically. Note that you're not sending a regular email; instead, you are sending the electronic equivalent of a greeting card.

Click

End

How-To Hints

Sending a Nonvirtual Card

If you don't think it's enough to send an electronic greeting card, you can send an actual (nonvirtual) card. Just click the **send a card** link in the search results window and go from there.

Getting More Information

After you track down a person using the White Pages, you can get more information about directions and what do to in the area by clicking the link to the right of **More Information**.

If You Don't Have a Full Name

If you're not sure how to spell a person's first name, try using an initial or the first few letters of the name. You must type the last name in full if the first name is abbreviated. You may also type in part of the last name if you type in a full first name.

How to Find Businesses Using the Yellow Pages

Trying to find a florist shop in Fort Bragg? Need to find the number of the hotel where you spent your last vacation? Whether you need local or across-the-country information, the Yellow Pages can make it easy for you to locate a business. Having access to AOL's Yellow Pages is just like having an entire United States Yellow Pages sitting next to your phone. But in these online Yellow Pages, you can look up a business not just by category, but also by name.

Begin

1 Choose Yellow Pages

Make sure that you're signed on to AOL. Click the **Internet** icon on the toolbar and choose **Yellow Pages**. The **AOL Yellow Pages** window opens.

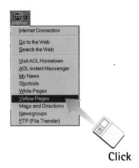

Click

2 Fill in the Information

Type a business category or a business name in the appropriate text box. You must also enter the state in which you want to start your search; you can enter the city as well if you want. When you've filled out the text boxes, click the **Find!** button.

Click

3 Choose a Subcategory

You may be able to narrow your search by choosing from one of several available subcategories. (For example, if you started by searching for **restaurants**, you might be able to go on to search for **Indian restaurants**.) To do this, just click the desired subcategory.

Click

4 Read the Results

An **AOL Yellow Pages Search Results** page appears with companies matching your query.

5 Get Directions

If you need to find out how to get to where you're going, click either the **map** or the **driving directions** link. A new page opens with a map and the location of your target business clearly shown.

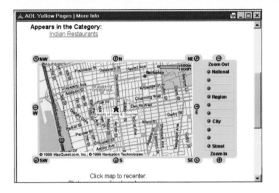

6 Perform Another Search

To search for another company (or to refine your search if you received too many matches), click the **AOL Yellow Pages** link and enter new search criteria.

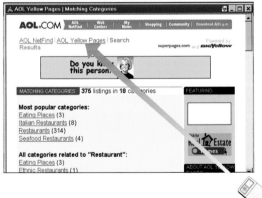

Click

End

How-To Hints

If You Don't Have a Full Name

If you're not sure of the complete name of the business, just type what you know; the search engine will try to finish the name.

Performing More Complex Searches

This task explained how to perform a simple search. AOL lets you perform much more complex searches as well. (Just click the various tabs—such as **Detailed Search** or **Distance Search**—available in the **AOL Yellow Pages** window shown in Step 1.) A detailed search lets you search for all the categories available in a simple search (business name or category, as well as city and state), plus keywords, a street name or address, zip code, and phone number. A distance search lets you search within a designated distance of a designated address. For example, you may want to find a restaurant that's within two miles of your home. You can also do a Canadian search or a search by category (such as **photographers** or **musical instruments**).

How to Read a Newsgroup

Newsgroups—also known as Usenet groups, Usenet news, and Internet news—are the Internet's equivalent of AOL message boards (see Part 3, "Communicating"). Despite the name, newsgroups contain online discussions rather than news. There are thousands upon thousands of newsgroups on topics ranging from dogs to volleyball to analyzing stock-market trends. With all these choices, it may seem like an overwhelming task just to get started with newsgroups. For this reason, AOL has already set up a list of selected newsgroups for you. This task describes how to read one of these newsgroups.

Begin

1 Choose Newsgroups

Make sure that you're signed on to AOL. Click the **Internet** icon in the toolbar and select **Newsgroups**. (If you haven't selected this option before, you may be told to choose a junk post-filtering option so that you aren't subjected to so many junk posts. See the How-To Hints for details on how to do this.) The **Newsgroups** window opens.

Click

2 Choose Read My Newsgroups

Click **Read My Newsgroups**. The **Read My Newsgroups** window opens, listing the newsgroups that AOL has set up for you and the number of total and unread messages contained within each group.

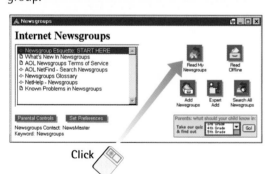

Click

3 Choose a Newsgroup to Read

Several of the newsgroups toward the top of this list—the ones whose names begin with **aol**—have been created by AOL to help you learn about newsgroups. These groups are local; they're shared only among AOL members. The remainder of the entries are true Internet newsgroups, shared across the Internet. Select any one of these groups and click **List Unread**.

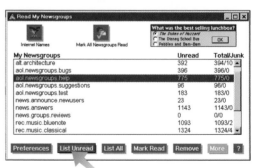

Click

4 Choose a Subject

Another window opens, listing your chosen newsgroup's **Subjects** and the **Number** of messages contained within each subject. Select a subject and click **List**. (To save a step and proceed directly to the selected subject's first message, you can click **Read** instead, and then skip to Step 6.)

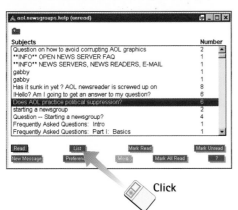

Click

5 Choose a Message

The next window you see lists your chosen subject's messages. Each item contains the message sender's Internet address and the date and time the message was posted. Select a message and click **Read Message**.

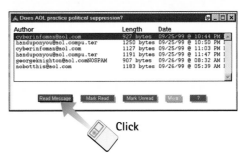

Click

6 Read the Message

Another window opens, displaying the message. When you've finished reading the message, click **Message-->** to display the next message, or **<--Message** to see the previous message, if there is one. (If you've already reached the current subject's last message, click **<<--Subject** to display the first message in the previous subject or **Subject-->>** to display the first message in the next subject.)

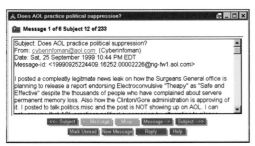

End

How-To Hints

Reading Messages You've Already Read

Unlike AOL message boards, newsgroups track the messages you have and have not read rather than the date you last visited a group. If you click **List Unread** (as shown in Step 3) when you visit a group, you'll see only unread messages. To review messages you've already read, click **List All** instead of **List Unread**.

Contributing to a Newsgroup

There are accepted conventions, know as *netiquette*, for posting messages to newsgroups. (To read up on netiquette, choose **Newsgroup Etiquette: START HERE** from the initial **Newsgroups** window.) Most newsgroups also have a list of Frequently Asked Questions (FAQs) to guide you on group etiquette. When you're familiar with these rules of behavior, try posting your own message. To do so, click a **New Message** or **Reply** button from anywhere within the newsgroup subject to which you want to post.

How to Add a Newsgroup

After you've read through the newsgroups that AOL has set up for you, you might want to start tapping into newsgroups that focus on particular topics that interest you. To do this more easily, you can add newsgroups to your **Read My Newsgroups** list. After you've added a newsgroup to this list, reading the group and posting messages to it are the same as for any of the newsgroups in your existing list. In this task, you learn how to add a newsgroup to your newsgroups list.

Begin

1 Choose Add Newsgroups

Open the **Newsgroups** window by clicking the **Internet** icon in the toolbar and selecting **Newsgroups**. From the **Newsgroups** window, click **Add Newsgroups**. The **Add Newsgroups-Categories** window opens.

Click

2 Choose a Newsgroup Category

This window lists the many available newsgroup categories and the number of topics contained within each category. Select one of these categories and then click **List**.

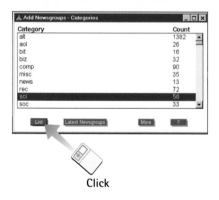

Click

3 Choose a Topic

The next window lists your chosen category's topics and the number of available newsgroups within each topic. Select a topic and then click **List**.

Click

4 Adding a Newsgroup

Now you'll see a window listing your chosen topic's newsgroups and the number of messages within each group. If you see a newsgroup that you want to add to your customized list, select that group and then click **Subscribe**. (Adding or joining a newsgroup is often called *subscribing* to that newsgroup.)

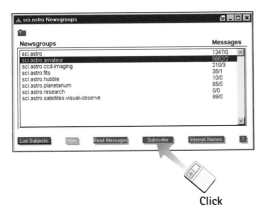

Click

6 Set Your Newsgroup Preferences

Now you're given the opportunity to choose your newsgroup preferences. You can determine the maximum length and age of newsgroup messages you'll be viewing. You can also set up filters to exclude certain types of messages. These settings affect only the selected newsgroup; you have to set your preferences for each newsgroup separately. When you're done, click **Save**. Now when you open your **Read My Newsgroups** window, your newly added newsgroup appears in the list. Use the steps in Task 7 to read and post messages to this group.

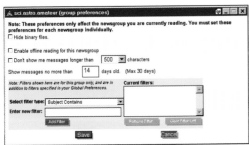

End

5 Confirm the Subscription

A dialog box informs you that you are now subscribed to the selected group. Click **OK** to close this dialog box.

Click

How-To Hints

Checking Out a Newsgroup

To review a newsgroup before adding it to your newsgroups list, click **List Subjects** or **Read Messages** in Step 4 before using the **Subscribe** button.

Other Ways of Adding Newsgroups

There are two additional ways to add newsgroups to your list. If you know the exact Internet name for a newsgroup (perhaps you've read about it in another group), you can use the **Expert Add** button in the **Newsgroups** window shown in Step 1. To search for newer newsgroups, click **Latest Newsgroups** in the **Add Newsgroups-Categories** window shown in Step 2; you'll see a list of newsgroups that have been added since the last time you clicked this button.

Removing a Newsgroup

To remove a newsgroup from your newsgroups list, select the group in your **Read My Newsgroups** window, click **Remove**, and then click **OK** in the resulting confirmation box.

How to Use Newsgroup Finder

If you're still not sure how to locate a newsgroup that meshes with your lifestyle, hobbies, or special interests, **Newsgroup Finder** can help. **Newsgroup Finder** helps you search through thousands of newsgroup articles for words or phrases key to the information or subject you're trying to track down. Whether you're looking for a job or you're curious whether anyone still has a pet rock, **Newsgroup Finder** can narrow your search to a few articles or groups.

Begin

1 Choose Search Newsgroups

Make sure that you're signed on to AOL. Open the **Newsgroups** window by clicking the **Internet** icon in the toolbar and choosing **Newsgroups**. From the **Newsgroups** window, double-click **AOL NetFind-Search Newsgroups**. The **AOL NetFind | Search Newsgroups** page opens.

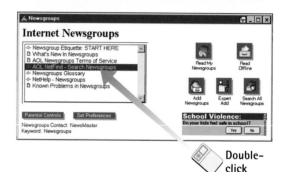

Double-click

2 Enter Your Search Criteria

Use this page to search for words in newsgroup articles (the actual message postings) or newsgroup descriptions (the places to find articles). For this example, leave the **newsgroup articles** radio button selected, type your search criterion in the text box, and click **Find!** to search the text of newsgroup articles for your search string.

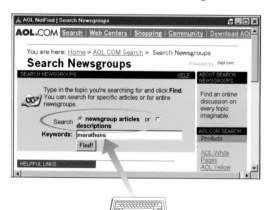

3 Search Newsgroups by Articles

A series of search results appears (you may have to scroll down to see them all). Each item in the list includes the message subject, the newsgroup it was posted to, when it was posted, and the author. Scroll through the page to find an interesting item. To read the newsgroup article, click the subject listing (it's a link). Use the **Previous** arrow on the AOL toolbar to return to the window shown in Step 2 so that you can search newsgroup descriptions.

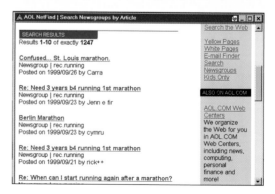

4 Search Newsgroups by Description

To search for newsgroups by description, click the **descriptions** radio button on the **AOL NetFind | Search Newsgroups** window, type your search criterion, and click the **Find!** button.

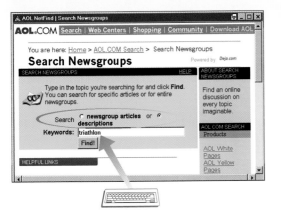

5 View the Search Results Page

The search results page displays a list of newsgroups that meet your search criterion. Click a newsgroup to see an expanded listing on your topic.

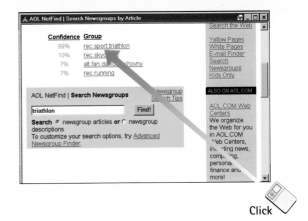

Click

6 Read the Articles

A new page opens with a list of articles similar to the page you saw in Step 3. Find one you're interested in and open it by clicking it.

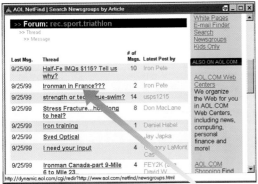

Click

End

How-To Hints

Using Multiple Search Criteria

When you type multiple words, **Newsgroup Finder** finds articles that include all the words in your search criteria (although not necessarily next to each other). This is the same as using an **AND** operator.

Customizing Your Find Options

Note that you can click **Advanced Newsgroup Finder** from the **AOL NetFind | Search Newsgroups** page to customize your find options.

Narrowing Your Search

You can use **OR** and **NOT** to change your search results. Refer to Task 12, "How to Search a Searchable Database," in Part 2. You can also narrow searches by using quotation marks to find phrases you want to find. For example, to find the phrase *Ironman Triathlon*, type "**Ironman Triathlon**".

How to Download Files with FTP

FTP (File Transfer Protocol) is an application commonly used on the Internet to transfer files from one computer to another. Hundreds of organizations on the Internet maintain public or anonymous FTP servers where people can access file archives. Internet file archives are full of information, images, and software, just like the software libraries on AOL. Downloading files from the Internet is similar to downloading files from AOL, with one catch: You have to know where the file is to download it. Of course, AOL has provided you with a solution to this snag: a search option right on the FTP window.

Begin

1 Search for an FTP Site

Make sure that you're signed on to AOL. Click the **Internet** icon in the toolbar and choose **FTP (File Transfer)** to display the **FTP–File Transfer Protocol** window. If you know the name of the FTP server on which the file you want to download is located, click **Go To FTP** and skip to Step 4. Otherwise, click **Search for FTP Sites**. An **FTP Search** window opens.

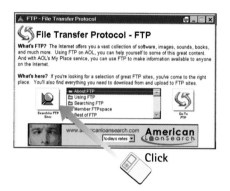

2 Enter Your Search Criteria

Type your search criteria in the text box and click **Search**. A list of FTP sites that contain files meeting your search criteria appears in the lower list box.

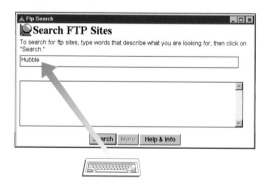

3 Write Down a Site Name

To find out whether the file you need is located at this site, write down the name of one or more sites, return to the window shown in Step 1 (to get there, close the **FTP Search** window by clicking its close button). Back in the **FTP–File Transfer Protocol** window, click **Go To FTP**. (Alternatively, double-click one of the site names in the **FTP Search** window to see a list of available files at that FTP site.) The **Anonymous FTP** window opens.

4 Select the Site

If your site is listed in the **Favorite Sites** list box, select the site, click **Connect**, and skip to Step 6. If your site is not listed, click **Other Site**. The **Other Site** dialog box opens.

Click

5 Enter the Site Address

In the **Site Address** text box, type the FTP site address you noted in Step 3 and click **Connect**.

6 Find and Download the File

The FTP software automatically logs you in as **anonymous** and provides you with a directory listing in the list box. (You may receive a warning that access restrictions apply.) Hunt through directories as needed to find your file. (You may need to trek through several directories to find the file you want; the directory structures on FTP sites may not be as intuitive as what you're used to.) When you find the file you want, select the filename and click **Download Now**. Select a location for the file in the **Download Manager** window. Click **Save** to accept the name and directory suggested and begin downloading your file.

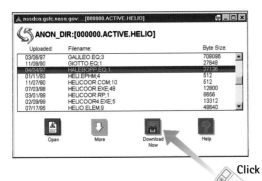

Click

How-To Hints

Logging In to an FTP Server

Public FTP servers use **anonymous** for the login name. The password is your email address. If you need to FTP to a server where you have an account, click the **Ask for Login Name and Password** check box shown in Step 5.

Navigating FTP Sites

FTP sites are not necessarily easy to navigate. Usually, the first directory you need to open on an anonymous FTP site is **pub**. If you're having difficulty finding a file, look for a Readme file or one named 1s-1R; these files often have information on file paths. (*Paths* are the directories or folders you need to open to get to a file.)

End

How to Find Maps and Get Directions

One of AOL 5's handiest new features lets you generate maps and driving directions in just minutes. No longer do you have to trek to the local book or travel store and dole out money for maps. In addition, in case you don't have a visual brain and have trouble reading maps, you can get door-to-door directions that are quite precise—often to tenths of miles if not less.

Begin

1 Choose Maps and Directions

Make sure that you're signed on to AOL. Click the **Internet** icon in the toolbar and choose **Maps and Directions**. The **Maps & Directions** window appears.

Click

2 Create a Map

From this window, you can get city and regional maps or state and international maps; you can map a U.S. address; and you can get driving directions. Try typing the name of a city and clicking **Create My Map**. (If you want, you can type a specific zip code instead.)

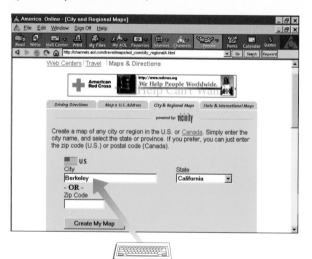

3 View Your Map

In a moment, you'll see a map of the designated city. Using the controls on the right side of the window, you can zoom in or out, or pan North, South, East, or West. You can also click anywhere within the map to center it around the spot you just clicked on.

4 Print Your Map

After you've zoomed, panned, and centered your map so that it's just the way you want it, you can print it. Click **Create a Printable Version**. Then choose **File, Print** from the menu bar, make any needed changes in the **Print** dialog box, and click **OK** to print the map.

Click

6 Read Your Directions

AOL generates both a map and a set of directions. As with your city map, you can get a printout by clicking **Create Printable Version** (scroll down to find this button) and then choosing **File, Print** from the menu bar.

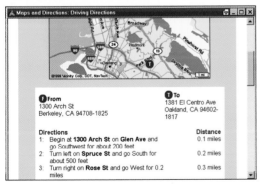

End

5 Get Directions

To get directions for how to drive from one place to another, click the **Driving Directions** tab of the **Maps & Directions** window. Type the address of your starting location, type the address of your destination location, and click **Get Directions**.

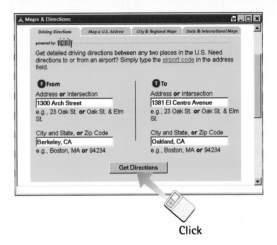

Click

How-To Hints

Creating State and International Maps

It's just as easy to create state and international maps as it is to create a city map. In the **Maps & Directions** window, click the **State & International Maps** tab. From this window, you can pick a state, a Canadian province, a country, or an international city for which you want a map. Then click **Go!** to generate the map.

Mapping a U.S. Address

You can map the area around any U.S. address. In the **Maps & Directions** window, click the **Map a U.S. Address** tab. From this window, type the address or intersection. Also provide either the city and state, or the zip code, but not both. Then click **Create My Map**.

Task

6

Sharing America Online with Your Family

*T*he tasks in this part help guide parents who want to introduce their family to AOL. In these tasks, you will learn how to share your AOL membership account with family members by setting up multiple screen names so that each member can have his or her own mailbox and individual password. You can establish degrees of access to AOL and the Internet so that each screen name has different access rights. You also learn how to control access to certain AOL areas—including email, Instant Messages, newsgroups, and more. Online activities are fun for your children; give yourself some peace of mind by allowing them to access only appropriate areas. ●

How to Set Up Multiple Screen Names

You might share your AOL account with your family in several ways. You could let them use your existing screen name and password, but then any one of them could receive (and even accidentally delete) your mail, send out messages bearing your name, and so on. You could also get a separate membership account for each family member, but the combined monthly membership fees could really add up. The best way to share your existing AOL membership account is by establishing unique screen names and passwords for up to seven members of your family under your single account. You can have all of that for the same monthly membership fee you pay for your individual account.

Begin

1 Choose Screen Names

Before signing on to AOL, ask each family member to provide a list of suggested screen names for his or her subaccount. Because each screen name must be unique to AOL, remind your family members to choose several alternative screen names. Sign on to AOL, click the **My AOL** toolbar icon, and select **Screen Names**. (Note that this procedure works only from the master account—the account you originally signed on to AOL with.)

Click

2 Choose a Screen Name

The **AOL Screen Names** window opens. Click **Create a Screen Name**. The **Create a Screen Name** windows opens.

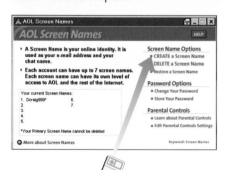

Click

3 Choose a Screen Name

Read the information on this page and click the **Create Screen Name** button to begin creating a screen name. In the **Choose a Screen Name** window, type a screen name for the subaccount and click **Continue**. (If the screen name you typed is already in use, AOL will request that you try another screen name and may suggest one for you.)

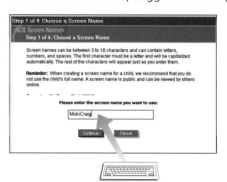

4 Enter a Password

Type a password for the new screen name in each of the two text boxes. Like your own password, this password can be four to eight characters long and should be something that's easy to remember, but not easy to guess. For security reasons, the password displays onscreen as asterisks. When you're done, click **Continue**.

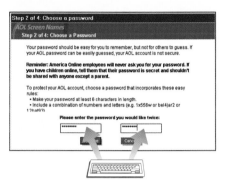

5 Set a Parental Controls Category

From this screen, select a parental controls category. You're basically setting an age group so that your child can access only appropriate material. (You'll learn how to change parental controls in Task 4, "How to Set Up Parental Chat Controls," later in this part). Click **Continue** to proceed.

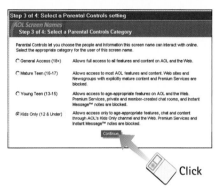

Click

6 Confirm Your Settings

A confirmation window informs you that the screen name has been added to your account. Click **Accept Settings** to accept the default settings for the account and close this dialog box. (You can also click **Customize Settings** to fine-tune the parental controls for this screen name. You'll learn more about parental controls in later tasks in this part.) You'll return to the **AOL Screen Names** window, in which the new screen name is listed.

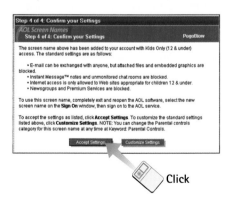

Click

End

How-To Hints

Signing On with a New Screen Name

After you've set up several screen names, it's easy to log on using any screen name for which you have the password. Pull down the **Select Screen Name** drop-down list (in either the **Sign On** or **Goodbye from America Online** window), click the desired screen name, enter the password for that screen name, and click **Sign On** or **Sign On Again**. (For the details on changing, as well as saving, passwords, see Task 3, "How to Change and Store Your Password.")

Changing a Parental Controls Category

From the master account, you can change a parental controls category by using the buttons at the bottom of the **Parental Controls** window, which is discussed in more depth in Tasks 4 through 6.

How to Switch Screen Names Online

The **Switch Screen Names** feature lets you switch between all the screen names in your account without signing off AOL and risking not being able to get another connection. If you just need to check your mail, the feature tells you which screen names have mail so that you don't switch if you don't have to. Parental controls are in effect when the new screen name signs in; you must use your password to switch to your screen name to make the process secure.

Begin

1 Choose Switch Screen Name

When you're ready to switch to another family member's account, click **Switch Screen Name** in the **Sign Off** menu.

Click

2 Review the Available Screen Names

The **Switch Screen Names** window opens, listing the master account and all sub-accounts. The **E-mail** column indicates whether a screen name has mail. (A colored envelope indicates that new mail has arrived; a white envelope indicates no new mail.)

3 Choose a Screen Name

Select the screen name you want to change to and click **Switch**.

Click

4 Note How Long You're Online

A dialog box informs you how long you've been online with the current screen name. Click **OK** to end your session using the current screen name and switch to the new screen name.

Click

5 Enter Your Password

A **Password** window opens. Type the password for the account you're switching to and click **OK**. (Keep in mind that you shouldn't share your password with family members if you don't want them to be able to switch over to your account.) You may not see this **Password** window if the password for this screen name has been stored, as described in the next task.

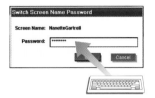

6 Use Your Account

AOL displays a **Welcome** window. (Depending on your level of access, you may see an additional screen such as this **Teens Welcome Screen**.) You are now ready to use your AOL account, just as if you'd used the **Sign On** window and dialed in yourself. To sign off AOL, choose **Sign Off** from the **Sign Off** menu or use the **Switch Screen Name** option to allow another member of your family to sign on.

End

How-To Hints

No Switching Between Master Accounts

You can only switch screen names between your master account and any of the sub-accounts you created within it. You cannot use the **Switch Screen Name** option to switch between separate master accounts.

Parental Controls

Parental controls for each account are listed in the right column in the **Switch Screen Name** window. Accounts listed as **General** do not have parental controls.

How to Change and Store Your Password

AOL 5 makes it easy to both change your password and store your password. In a sense, these two actions have the opposite effect. Storing your password makes it easier to access your account. This can be convenient, but may not be a wise idea if several people using different screen names are sharing one AOL account—it makes your account less secure. On the other hand, if you want to keep your account more secure, changing your password on a regular basis is an excellent practice.

Begin

1 Choose Passwords

To change your password, click the **My AOL** icon on the toolbar and choose **Passwords**. An informational screen about passwords opens.

Click

2 Read About Changing Passwords

To change the password for the screen name you're currently signed on as, click the **Change Password** button. The **Change Your Password** screen appears.

Click

3 Change Your Password

Type your old password in the **Old password** text box and type your new password twice in the **Enter new password twice** text boxes (the second time as confirmation). Click **Change Password**.

Click

4 Confirm the Change

You'll receive notification that your password has been changed. In addition, if you've stored your password, you must change it (see the next step for details). Click **OK** to close the confirmation box.

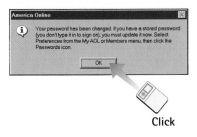

Click

5 Choose Password Preferences

To store your password, click the **My AOL** icon on the toolbar, choose **Preferences**, and double-click the **Passwords** icon in the **Preferences** window. (This process is the same whether you're storing your password for the first time or updating a stored password after changing your password, as just described.)

 Double-click

6 Store Your Password

In the **Store Passwords** dialog box that appears, type your current password in the text box. Choose whether to have the password stored for sign-on, for access to your Personal Filing Cabinet (PFC), or both. If you do not store your password for PFC, you must type your password whenever you try to open your Personal Filing Cabinet. Click **OK** to store the password. The next time you log on or access your Personal Filing Cabinet, you won't have to type your password.

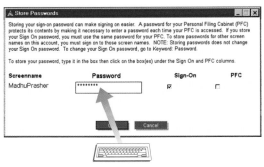

End

How-To Hints

The Risks of Storing Passwords

If you store the passwords of any accounts or subaccounts, anyone can switch to those accounts without providing the password—and can potentially read your email, muck around in your Personal Filing Cabinet, and more. In other words, if you share your AOL account with friends or family members, it's best not to store your password.

Who Can Change and Store Passwords

You can change your password only if the parental controls on your account have been set to **General** or **Mature Teen**. You can store your password only if your account has been set to at least **Young Teen**.

How to Set Up Parental Chat Controls

After you've explored AOL's areas, you'll realize that AOL can be a valuable part of your children's education. Like any community, however, AOL's electronic community may provide experiences you don't want your kids to undergo. One of these is the use of foul, abusive, or suggestive language in unmonitored chat rooms. Although AOL expressly forbids such language, it unfortunately does occur. If this concerns you, you may want to set up parental chat controls on any or all of your children's subaccounts to prevent them from visiting certain chat rooms.

Begin

1 Choose Parental Controls

You set up chat controls in the **Parental Control** area. Make sure that you're signed on to AOL (with the master account), click the **My AOL** icon on the toolbar, and choose **Parental Controls**. The **AOL Parental Controls** window opens.

Click

2 Choose Custom Controls

Click **Set Parental Controls**. The **Parental Controls** window opens.

Click

3 Choose Chat

You can set controls for several features from this window. You'll learn about some of the other areas in the next few tasks. For now, select the account for which you want to set up parental controls from the **Edit controls for** list box at the top of the window. Then click **Chat control**.

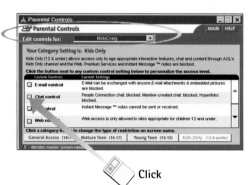
Click

4 Choose Chat Controls

A **Custom Control Settings: Chat** window opens. From here, you can choose whether to block out several different categories of chat rooms. **Block People Connection-featured chat rooms** prevents entrance to any People Connection chat rooms. **Block member-created public and private chat rooms** prevents entrance to any member-created People Connection chat rooms. **Block all non-People Connection chat rooms** prevents entrance to any chat room outside the People Connection channel. Obviously, the more check boxes you select, the more limited your child's exposure will be to chat rooms.

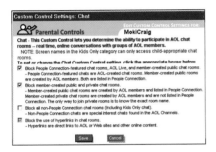

5 Saving Chat Controls

When you're done making selections, click the **Save** button. You'll see a confirmation dialog box. Click **OK** to proceed.

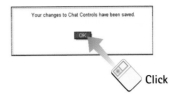

Click

6 Blocked Features

If a family member tries to use a feature you've blocked from his or her account, this dialog box indicates that the feature is blocked. In some cases, the menu option for the blocked feature is just not available to that screen name. For example, if you have **Kids Only** privileges, the **People** menu is not even available. Click **OK** to close the dialog box and continue with your AOL session.

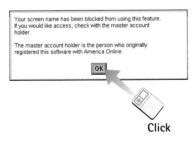

Click

End

How-To Hints

Setting Chat Controls for Other Screen Names

Remember that the procedure described here sets chat controls for a single screen name. To set chat controls for additional screen names, follow the steps outlined here, but choose a different screen name in Step 3.

Handling Inappropriate Behavior

If you or someone in your family encounters inappropriate language or any other terms-of-service violations in a People Connection chat room, use the **Notify AOL** button. (See Task 3, "How to Use Chat Features," in Part 4 for details.)

How to Set Up Email Controls

Like chat controls, email controls can protect your children in their online experience. Internet mail enables children around the world to communicate more quickly and easily than ever before—but this form of communication can leave children vulnerable. AOL's mail controls enable parents to set specific controls on email addresses that young readers may or may not access. For example, you can prevent a specific screen name from receiving email attachments, from receiving non-AOL email, or from receiving email from particular email addresses.

Begin

1 Choose Parental Controls

As with chat controls, you set up email controls in the **Parental Control** area. Make sure that you're signed on to AOL (with the master account name), click the **My AOL** icon on the toolbar, and choose **Parental Controls**. In the **AOL Parental Controls** window, click **Set Parental Controls**. The **Parental Controls** window opens.

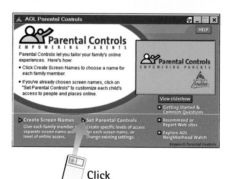

Click

2 Choose Email Control

In the **Edit controls for** list box, select the screen name for which you want to set up parental controls. Then click **E-mail control**.

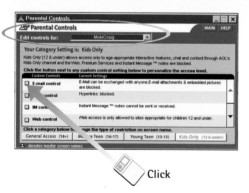

Click

3 Review Existing Mail Controls

A **Mail Controls** window for the selected individual opens. By default, each screen name can receive mail from any person anywhere in the world (because the **Allow all e-mail** option button is selected). Depending on the level of parental controls set on the account, file attachments and pictures may be blocked automatically.

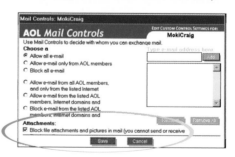

4 Set Mail Controls

Use the radio buttons on the left to allow or block mail. At the most extreme, you can block all email. You can also allow email from AOL members but block all other mail. There are also three options for selectively allowing or blocking addresses that you enter into the **Type e-mail address here** text box on the right. (Just type the email address and click the **Add** button.) In this example, MokiCraig can receive email from everyone except for those listed on the right.

5 Blocking Attachments

If you do not want this screen name to be able to receive mail attachments, make sure that you check the **Block file attachments and pictures in mail** check box. Note that this option is turned on by default for children and young teens (you can turn it off for them if you like). Mature teens and those with General access can receive attachments by default.

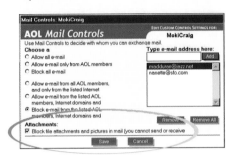

6 Save Your New Settings

When you have finished making changes in this window, click **Save**. You'll see a confirmation message that mail controls have been set. Click **OK** to return to the **Parental Controls** window. (If you're done setting controls, click the close button in the **Parental Controls** window.)

Click

End

How-To Hints

Setting Email Controls for Other Screen Names

The procedure described here sets email controls for a single screen name only. To set email controls for additional screen names, follow the steps outlined here but choose a different screen name in Step 2.

Removing Email Addresses to be Blocked/Allowed

In the **Mail Controls** window, you can create a list of email addresses to be blocked or allowed. (Whether they're blocked or allowed depends on which radio button you've chosen on the left.) If you change your mind about someone, it's simple enough to remove that name from the list: Just select the name and click the **Remove** button. To wipe out the entire list, click the **Remove All** button. When you're done, click **Save** to put your changes into place.

How to Set Up Instant Message and Web Controls

Instant Message and Web controls are similar to chat controls. Their purpose is to prevent your children from accessing information you don't want them to see or from engaging in dialogs you think may not be appropriate.

Begin

1 Choose Parental Controls

Make sure that you're signed on to AOL (with the master account name). Click the **My AOL** icon on the toolbar and choose **Parental Controls**. The **AOL Parental Controls** window opens.

Click

2 Set Parental Controls

Click **Set Parental Controls**. The **Parental Controls** window opens.

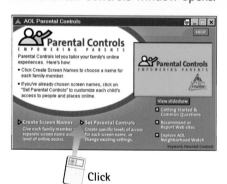

Click

3 Choose Instant Message Control

From the **Edit controls for** list box, select the screen name for which you want to set up parental controls. Then click **IM control**. (Just in case you can't remember, IM is short for Instant Message.) A **Custom Control Settings: Instant Messages** window opens.

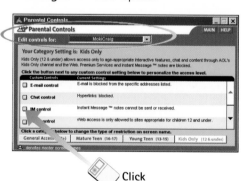

Click

4 Choose the Instant Message Setting

By default, Instant Messages are blocked for those with parental controls categories of **Kids Only** and **Young Teen**; Instant Messages are not blocked for other categories. You can select or de-select this check box as you see fit. Click **Save** when you're done, and click **OK** to respond to the confirmation dialog box.

Click

5 Choose Web Control

In the **Parental Controls** window, if necessary, select the screen name for which you want to set up parental controls. Then click **Web control**. A **Custom Control Settings: Web** window opens.

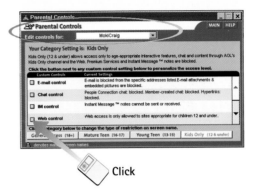

Click

6 Choose the Web Control Setting

Notice that the default level of access to the Web is determined by the parental control categories of the designated screen name. For example, a screen name under the parental control category of **Kids Only** automatically has the most limited Web access—that is, the **Access sites appropriate for ages 12 and under** option is selected. You can change the level of access as desired. Click **Save** when you're done, and click **OK** when you see the confirmation dialog box.

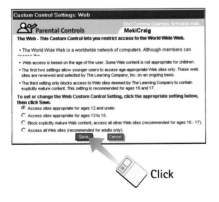

Click

How-To Hints

Web Sites Approved for Children

Web sites that AOL has approved for kids and teens are monitored to ensure that they continue to be suitable for the selected age group.

Talk to Your Kids

As in real life, setting up some rules and regulations is a good start, but is no substitute for talking to your kids. Depending on their age and maturity level, it's a good idea to explain why you're limiting their online experience, outline the possible hazards of certain types of online interactions, and so on.

End

How to Set Up Download and Newsgroup Controls

Newsgroups from the Internet are not covered by AOL's Terms of Service and may contain subjects and language not appropriate for children. But many newsgroups provide educational or entertaining reading material, so you may not want to block them out entirely. Newsgroup controls enable you to block all access, or only partial access, to possibly problematic newsgroups. Similarly, you may decide to limit your child's ability to download files. Downloading files exposes you to the risk of viruses. Besides, it's not out of the question that the files contain inappropriate material.

Begin

1 Choose Parental Controls

Make sure that you're signed on to AOL (with the master account name), click the **My AOL** icon on the toolbar, and then choose **Parental Controls**. The **AOL Parental Controls** window opens.

Click

2 Set Parental Controls

Click **Set Parental Controls**. The **Parental Controls** window opens.

Click

3 Choose Newsgroup

From the **Edit controls for** list box, select the screen name for which you want to set up parental controls. Then click **Newsgroup**. (You will need to scroll down using the arrows on the right to see this option.) A **Custom Control Settings: Newsgroups** window opens.

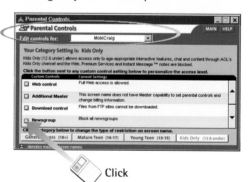

Click

4 Choose the Newsgroup Settings

Screen names with **Kids Only** access automatically have all newsgroups blocked, so the other options are grayed out. To make a different selection, first deselect the **Block all newsgroups** check box, then select the other check boxes as desired. For example, you can block all adult-content newsgroups as well as those having to do with games, as in this example. When you're done, click **Save** to put your changes into place.

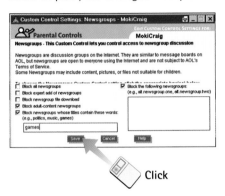

Click

5 Choose Download Control

In the **Parental Controls** window, select the screen name for which you want to set up parental controls, if necessary. Then click **Download control**. A **Custom Control Settings: Downloading Files** window opens.

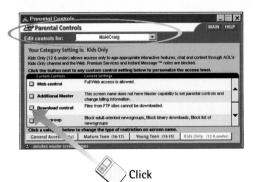

Click

6 Choose the Download Settings

Turning on the **Block FTP Downloads** option prevents the receipt of file downloads from Internet sites that use FTP (File Transfer Protocol). (Screen names with **Kids Only** access are automatically blocked from FTP downloads.) The **Block AOL Software Library Downloads** option prevents the receipt of file downloads from AOL software libraries. When you're done choosing whether and how to block downloads, click **Save** to save these settings.

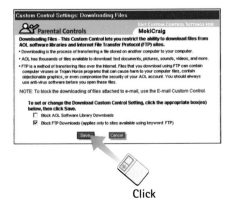

Click

How-To Hints

Using FTP

For more on the wilds of FTP—what it is, how it works, how to find files—consult Task 10, "How to Download Files with FTP," in Part 5.

Antivirus Programs

If you're downloading lots of files, especially files from the Internet, it's a good idea to protect yourself against viruses by installing a good antivirus program. You can buy antivirus programs at office stores and software stores; you can also use a search engine to search for antivirus programs to download.

End

How to Handle Junk Mail

If you hang out on AOL for long enough, there's a good chance you'll start to get a fair—or intolerable—amount of junk mail. Luckily, AOL provides a number of ways to filter your email, letting you discard mail from certain sites before it reaches your mailbox. This feature is available to AOL members to remove unsolicited email (not so fondly known as *spam*). If you, like many AOL members, do not want to receive such unsolicited mail, AOL requests your assistance to identify junk mail sources. Reducing junk mail reduces problems with your mailbox, which, if it becomes too full, could actually refuse mail you *want* to receive.

Begin

1 Choose Mail Controls

Make sure that you're signed on to AOL. Click the **Mail Center** toolbar icon and choose **Mail Controls**. The **Mail Controls** window opens.

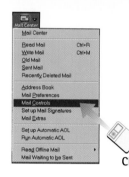

Click

2 Choose Junk Mail

For information on how to help AOL stop junk mail, click **Junk Mail**. The **Junk Mail** window appears.

 Click

3 Choose Report Junk Mail

For information about how to deal with junk email, click **Report Junk Mail**. The **Reporting Junk Email** window opens.

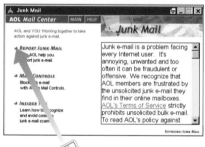

 Click

4 Read About Reporting Junk Mail

Scroll as necessary to read the document. Note that if you receive unsolicited email, you should forward it to the screen name **TOSSpam**. (Do not reply to the mail, even to tell senders to stop sending you mail; that only encourages them.) When you're done reading the document, click the close box to close the window.

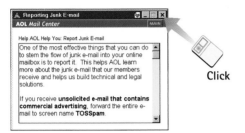

Click

5 Choose Insider Tips

For other information and helpful tips on dealing with junk mail, return to the **Junk Mail** window. Click **Insider Tips**.

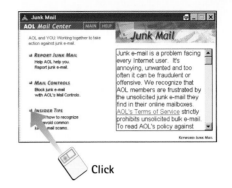

Click

6 Read About Avoiding Junk Mail

The **Recognizing and Avoiding Junk Email** window has many links to information and answers to questions about junk mail. Double-click one of the entries to find out more.

Double-click

End

How-To Hints

Unsolicited Commercial Email

If you receive unsolicited commercial advertising, click the **Forward** button in your email window and forward the message to the address **TOSSpam** (the text of the original message is forwarded, even though you don't see it in the mail window). The AOL Terms of Service staff will take the appropriate action to stop unsolicited commercial email.

Blocking Mail from Individuals

If you receive unwanted mail from an individual, use mail controls to block messages from that person's address. Refer to Task 5, "How to Set Up Email Controls," earlier in this part, for assistance.

How to Use the Reminder Service

AOL provides a convenient reminder service to jog your memory about important dates such as birthdays and anniversaries. Just enter the important names and dates, and AOL will send you a reminder email a few weeks before the big event. Whether you have an incurably bad memory or are just impossibly busy—like so many of us these days—these reminders can save you some embarrassment and keep you in everyone's good graces. Best of all, this service is completely free.

Begin

1 Choose Reminder Service

Make sure that you're signed on to AOL. Click the **My AOL** icon in the toolbar and choose **Reminder Service.** The **Reminder Service** window appears.

Click

2 Create a Reminder

Click **Create Your Reminder.** The **Holiday Reminder** window opens.

Click

3 Enter Your Information

Enter your name and sex in the **Holiday Reminder** window. You can also choose whether you want to receive a second reminder closer to the event. Select check boxes for the specific holidays—such as Valentine's Day and Mother's Day—you want to be reminded about. When you're ready, click **Continue**.

Click

4 Check Your Reminders

A list of your reminders appears. Click **Add Personal Reminder** to add a reminder that's relevant to a specific person—such as a partner or a boss. (If you want to add another holiday you forgot to select the first time around, click **Holiday Reminders**.)

Click

5 Add a Personal Reminder

In the **Add a Reminder Here** window, type the person's name, the name of the occasion, the date, and, optionally, the person's age and sex. When you're done entering information, click the **Save** button to add the item to your list of reminders. AOL adds the reminder and redisplays your list of reminders as a confirmation. From here, repeat Steps 4 and 5 to add additional reminders.

 Click

6 Editing and Removing Reminders

To edit a reminder, select it from the list and click the **Edit** button. You'll see the **Edit a Reminder Here** window, which is exactly like the **Add a Reminder Here** window except for its name. Make any necessary changes and click **Save**. If you decide to delete a reminder, select it from the list and click the **Remove** button. In the **Remove Reminder?** dialog box, click **OK** to go ahead with the deletion.

Click

End

How-To Hints

Is It Free?

Why is the personal reminder service free? In truth, AOL is hoping the service will induce you to go on an electronic shopping spree. The **Shopping Main** button at the bottom of the initial **Reminder Service** window leads you to AOL's **Shopping** channel—a sort of electronic shopping mall. In addition, when you receive your reminder, it includes a list of shopping suggestions, complete with handy links to sites where you can buy gifts. (You'll learn more about AOL's **Shopping** channel in Part 8, "Travel and Entertainment Channels.")

The Holidays

Unfortunately, AOL's list of holidays is limited to those shown in Step 3. However, you can always create your own individual holiday reminders using the **Add Personal Reminder** button.

10

How to Stay Safe Using Neighborhood Watch

You've already learned several ways to use parental controls to ensure that your child's online experience is a safe one. If you want to further educate yourself about online safety, consult AOL's **Neighborhood Watch**. This feature provides information about email safety (such as warding off junk mail and avoiding email scams), computer safety (protecting yourself from viruses), and more. The online world can be a bit of a jungle (you know this if you've visited even a few chat rooms), so it's best to venture out there properly equipped to take care of yourself.

Begin

1 Choose Parental Controls

Make sure that you're signed on to AOL. Click the **My AOL** icon in the toolbar and choose **Parental Controls**. The **AOL Parental Controls** window opens. (You can only get here if your parental controls level is **Mature Teen** or above.)

Click

2 Go to AOL Neighborhood Watch

Click the **Explore AOL Neighborhood Watch** button in the lower-right corner of the **Parental Controls** window. The **AOL Neighborhood Watch** window opens.

Click

3 Explore Neighborhood Watch

You can click the **Parental Controls** link to open the **Parental Controls** window, from which you can shape your child's online experience, as you learned in earlier tasks in this part. (To do so, you must be signed on with the master account name.) For this task, click **Email Safety** to read up on email safety and computer safety.

Click

4 Read about Email Safety

From this window, you can find out about setting up email controls, reducing junk mail, avoiding email scams, and so on. Click some topics to educate yourself more thoroughly about email safety. Click the close button to close a window when you're done reading.

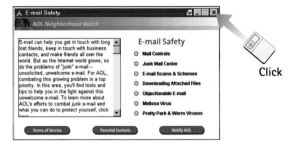

Click

5 Learn about Computer Safety

Back in the **AOL Neighborhood Watch** window, click **Computer Safety** to bring up this window. From here, you can learn a lot about viruses and Trojan horse programs—the better to protect yourself and your children from them. Click the various topics to find out more about computer safety. In particular, you may want to investigate the **Computer Protection Center**, which contains a wealth of information about viruses and also offers virus-protection software you can download in case you don't already have protection.

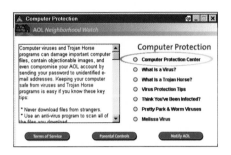

6 Safeguard Yourself and Your Kids

Back in the **AOL Neighborhood Watch** window, click **Suggested Safeguards** to display this window. From here, you can garner a great deal of information about password and privacy protection. For a quick and easy-to-understand list of safety tips to share with your kids, check out **Kids Online Safety Tips**.

End

How-To Hints

Notifying AOL

You've seen **Notify AOL** buttons in several other areas of AOL (you can click this button to report inappropriate behavior in chat rooms and so on). Click the **Notify AOL** button in the **AOL Neighborhood Watch** window if you want to lodge complaints of any type: about problems with Instant Messages, message boards, chat rooms, and more.

Safely Shopping and Banking Online

To read about safety for online shopping and banking, click the **Shopping & Banking** button in the **AOL Neighborhood Watch** window.

Task

News and Information Channels

*U*nlike some Internet service providers (ISPs), AOL provides *content* as well as email and access to the Internet. Channels are AOL's main content areas. You can access information on AOL from many different locations; AOL's channels help you locate information easily by topic. The tasks in this part will teach you how to use the channels that focus on news and information. Although many of AOL's channels include news, this part introduces you to the channels whose main purposes are keeping you informed about events in the news, maintaining your finances, and educating yourself. Before you dive into the news, you'll learn some general strategies for making your way around the various channels. ●

How to Browse AOL's Channels

Channels are the topic areas AOL has set up to help direct you to information. Channel topics range from computers to sports to music to education to research. Channels can help you locate games, find a job, meet people with common interests, and much more. Certain elements are available in more than one channel for your convenience. For example, most channels have a **Search and Explore** feature.

Begin

1 Display the Welcome Window

A **Welcome** window greets you each time you sign on to AOL. If the **Welcome** window is not currently displayed, bring it into view by clicking the **Channels** toolbar button and choosing **Welcome**.

Click

2 Choose a Channel

The left side of the **Welcome** window lists AOL's channels. As you learned earlier, you can access a channel simply by clicking its channel button. To experiment, click **Computing**. The **AOL Computing** window opens; this channel provides a wide range of computer-related resources.

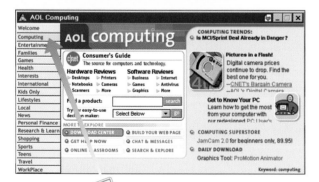

Click

3 Pick a Topic

When you're in a channel window, you can click any topic that interests you to get more information on the subject. For example, if you click **Computing Superstore**, you'll jump to this window, from which you can buy almost any imaginable piece of hardware or software. When you're done with a window, click its close button to return to the **AOL Computing** window.

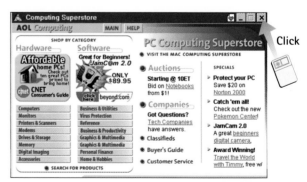

Click

4 Move to Another Channel

Moving from one AOL channel to another is easy—just click the button for the desired channel on the left side of the window. If you click the **Entertainment** button, for example, you see this **AOL Entertainment** window, which supplies late-breaking news about television, movies, music, and your favorite celebrities.

5 Learn More About a Channel

To preview what's available in a particular channel, hold your mouse pointer over the channel button. A box appears, listing some of the major topics within the channel. For example, if you point to the **Interests** button, you'll see this display.

6 Going Directly to a Channel

If you know which channel you want, but the channel buttons are not displayed, you can click the **Channels** icon in the toolbar and choose the channel you want to go directly to.

Click

End

How-To Hints

Getting to the Welcome Window

Occasionally, when you sign on, the **Welcome** window may be covered up by another window—often some sort of promotional offering. If you're interested, by all means read up on the offer (you may have to click the **Tell Me More!** button). Most likely, however, you'll want to clear the promotional window from view so that you can get to your trusty **Welcome** window. Typically, you do this by clicking the **No Thanks** button.

Other Ways to Access Channels

You can also access each channel by keyword, or you can keep channels in your Favorites list.

How to Get 24-Hour News

Suppose that you want to read today's news. Are you interested in news in general, or maybe something more specific, such as business, sports, or weather? Perhaps national or world news is more to your liking. AOL is ready for you on all counts. Whenever you're online, the **News** channel is available 24 hours a day, ad-free, with up-to-the-minute news. Whether you're looking for news highlights or in-depth reports, today's news is just a few clicks away.

Begin

1 Choose the News Channel

Make sure that you're signed on to AOL, and then click the **News** button in the channel bar in the **Welcome** window. (You can also click the **Channels** icon in the toolbar and choose **News**.) The **Today's News** window opens.

Click

2 Choose a Top Story

The news marquee changes as the events of the day unfold. The latest news stories appear under **Top Stories**. Click a top story to read about it. A window displays the text of the story you clicked.

Click

3 Read a Top Story

Use the scrollbar as needed to read the information in the text window. To change to a different news department, click one of the buttons underneath the **AOL News** heading in the upper-left corner of the window (such as **Business**, **Politics**, or **Weather**).The list of headlines changes accordingly. To experiment, click the **U.S. & World** button.

Click

4 Choose an Article

From the **U.S. and World News** window, you can choose an article to read, or you can switch to yet another news area by clicking another one of the buttons—**Local**, **Sports**, and so forth—in the upper-left corner of the window.

Click

5 Choose a Newspaper or Magazine

If you don't want to read just any old article but want to choose which periodical you're reading, visit AOL's newsstand. From the main **News** window, click **Newsstand** (you can return to the main **News** window by clicking the **Main** button near the top of the current article window). In the **Newsstand For News** window that appears, you can choose to read from such periodicals as *The New York Times*, *Newsweek*, *Atlantic Monthly*, the *Christian Science Monitor*, and others.

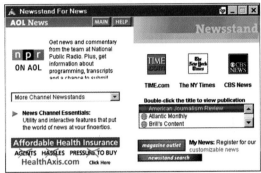

End

How-To Hints

Searching for News

To access a searchable database of news articles, click the **Search** button in the main **News** window (or type the keyword **news search**). Refer to Part 2, "America Online Features," for information on using searchable databases.

Creating a News Profile

If you don't want to go hunting for news but instead want the news to come to you, you can set up a news profile. Flip back to Task 10, "How to Set Up Your AOL News Profile," in Part 2 for details.

How to Check the Weather Forecast

Is it going to rain tomorrow? What kind of weather can you expect on your upcoming weekend trip? Weather can be critical news to you, but unless the weather is especially severe or unusual, general weather forecasts outside your area rarely make it on the local news. To see general weather forecasts, you can visit AOL's **Weather** area. You'll find five-day weather forecasts for just about every major city in the world, and these forecasts are available 24 hours a day. So the next time you're wondering whether you should walk out of the house in a slicker or a swimsuit, ask AOL.

Begin

1 Choose the News Channel

Make sure that you're signed on to AOL and click the **News** button on the left side of the **Welcome** window. The **Today's News** window opens.

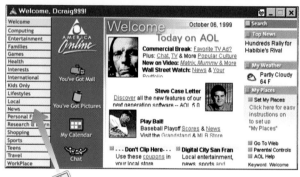

 Click

2 Choose the Weather Department

Click the **Weather** button. The **National Weather** window opens.

Click

3 Choose an Area

In the **Search** text box at the top of the window, type an area code, zip code, city, or state and click **Search**.

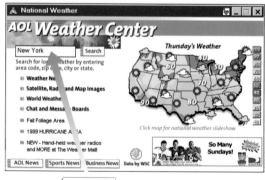

4 Pick the Location

The **Search Results** window displays the areas that meet your search criteria. Double-click an item in this window to see weather details about this particular area. A weather forecast window opens for the area you selected.

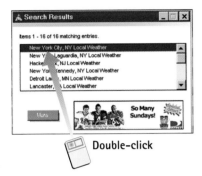

Double-click

5 Read the Weather Report

Current conditions are displayed on the left side of the window. For more weather information, read the text box on the right. If you're fascinated by weather pictures, click **Satellite, Radar and Map Images**. The **Weather Images** window opens.

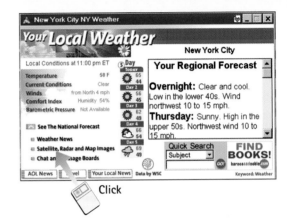

Click

6 Find Weather Maps and Images

Click the **Satellite**, **Radar**, or **Maps** tab and then hunt for the images you want to view.

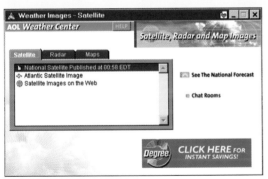

End

How-To Hints

More About Weather

To get a more in-depth picture of the weather, go to the **National Weather** window (see Step 3) and choose from the available options, such as **Weather News** and **World Weather**.

Talk About the Weather

The **National Weather** window also gives you access to chat and message boards so that you can discuss the weather with other AOL members. Click the **Chat and Message Boards** item in the **National Weather** window (shown in Step 3) to visit these areas.

How to Track Your Stock

Do you own stock, mutual funds, or bonds? Are you interested in monitoring how an investment (or potential investment) is doing? If so, check out AOL's **Quotes** and **Portfolios** areas. They are updated frequently during each business day and include a wealth of information—from current prices to price/earnings (P/E) ratios.

Begin

1 Choose Personal Finance

Make sure that you're signed on to AOL and click the **Personal Finance** button on the left side of the **Welcome** window. (You can also click the **Channels** icon in the toolbar and choose **Personal Finance**.) The **AOL Personal Finance** window opens.

Click

2 Choose Quotes

Under **Quotes, Charts, News & Research**, make sure that **Quote Center** is selected and click **Go**. The **AOL Investment Snapshot** window opens.

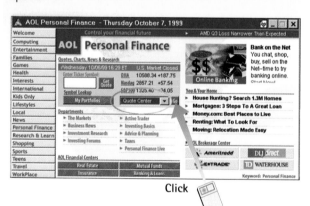

Click

3 Enter the Stock Symbol or Name

This window provides a variety of options for retrieving stock information. (You can go directly to this window by clicking the **Quotes** icon in the toolbar.) Every publicly traded stock has a unique stock symbol—an abbreviation of the company's name. If you know it, type the symbol for the desired stock in the text box; if you don't know the symbol, click the **Name** radio button and type the company's name instead. Then click **Get Quote**.

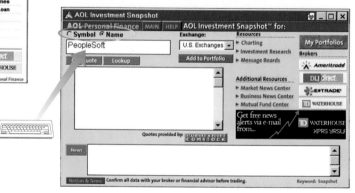

4 Read Your Stock Quote

If AOL recognizes your stock symbol or the company name, the list box displays that stock's current quote. (The company's symbol appears to the left of its name, in case you didn't already know it.) If AOL doesn't recognize the symbol you entered, select the company for which you want a stock quote from the **Lookup Results** window that opens and click **Select**. To get an additional quote, delete your stock symbol from the text box and repeat Step 3.

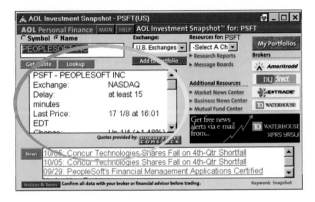

5 Create an Online Portfolio

To have AOL add a selected stock to an online portfolio, display a stock quote for that company (as you did in Step 4) and click **Add to Portfolio**. You'll see the **Add to Portfolio** window, listing the stock's symbol and exchange. You can enter the price per share and number of shares. (You can enter real or fictitious information here, whichever you prefer.) When you're done, click **OK** to add the stock to your portfolio. Click **OK** again at the confirmation window.

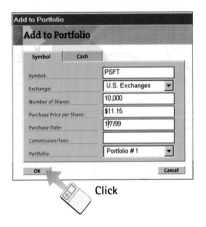

Click

6 View Your Portfolio

You'll see a **Portfolio** window listing all the stocks (real or hypothetical) in your portfolio. You can also open the **Portfolio** window by clicking the **My Portfolios** button in the **Personal Finance** window (shown in Step 2). From the **My Portfolios** window, double-click the portfolio you want to open, or click the **Help** button for more information on creating your own portfolio.

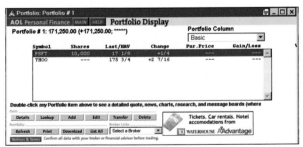

End

How-To Hints

Remember Stock Symbols

After you find a stock symbol, make a note of it. If you know the symbol, you can quickly get a stock quote by entering the symbol in the **Enter Ticker Symbol** text box in the initial **AOL Personal Finance** window and then clicking **Get Quote**.

Buying Stocks Online

You can also buy real stocks with real money. Click **AOL Brokerage Center** in the lower-right corner of the initial **AOL Personal Finance** window for information on AOL's online brokerage firms.

How to Research Mutual Funds

Do you feel intimidated by the stock market? If so, you may prefer to invest in mutual funds rather than in individual stocks. Fortunately, AOL provides easy access to a wealth of information about mutual funds. As you'll see, it's just as simple to check how a particular fund of yours is performing as it is to carry out some research on what might be the best funds for you to buy.

Begin

1 Choose Personal Finance

Make sure that you're signed on to AOL and click the **Personal Finance** button on the left side of the **Welcome** window. (You can also click the **Channels** icon in the toolbar and choose **Personal Finance**.) When the **AOL Personal Finance** window opens, click **Mutual Funds**. The **Mutual Fund Center** window opens.

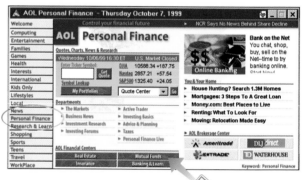

Click

2 Look Up Funds

From this window, you can access a wealth of information about mutual funds, go to a fund-trading service, and even chat about mutual funds. To find out about a particular fund, type its symbol in the text box under **Search Reports by Symbol** and press **Enter** (then jump to Step 5). If you don't know the fund symbol, click **Lookup Funds** to find the fund by name.

Click

3 Choose a Fund Family

In the **Mutual Fund Names List** page that appears, scroll until you find the name of the fund family you're interested in (say, **Scudder**) and click it.

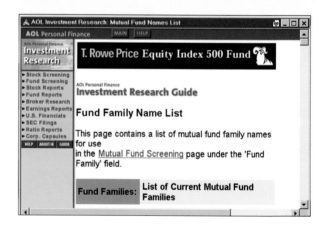

4 Choose a Fund

You'll see a list of funds in the family you selected. Click the particular fund you're interested in. (Note that each fund's symbol is listed to the left of its name. Jot down this symbol; it will help you find information about the fund more quickly in the future.)

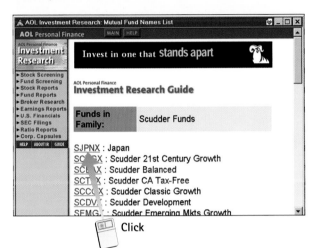

Click

5 Choose Investment Snapshot

In the **Search Results** window that appears, click **AOL Investment Snapshot**.

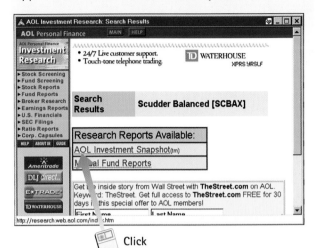

Click

6 Check the Fund's Performance

You'll see a quick picture of this fund's current value and recent performance. You can also click **Mutual Fund Reports** in the **Search Results** window shown in Step 5 for more detailed information.

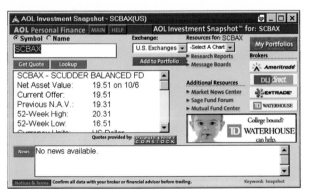

 End

How-To Hints

Fund Screening

If you don't want to look up funds by name but prefer to hunt for funds that meet particular criteria (those that have a high enough return, for example), you can use AOL's fund-screening feature. From the **Mutual Fund Center** window (shown in Step 2), click the **Fund Screening** button. Then choose between step-by-step screening and custom fund screening, depending on how investment savvy you are. (If you lose your way, you can always click the **Help** button for assistance.)

If you're a novice at investing and the fund-screening process seems too overwhelming, it's easy to get more specific advice on which funds might be right for you. For starters, try clicking **Sage** for invaluable advice on making sense of mutual funds. You can also click the **Top Funds List** for a list of funds reviewed and endorsed (for the moment) by the experts.

How to Start Your Own Business in WorkPlace

Have you ever wondered about owning your own business? Curious about what it would take to get started? For help on these and more questions about starting a business, visit the **WorkPlace** channel and find out what being a business owner is all about. The **WorkPlace** channel even has information to help you figure out what kind of business you'd be best at.

Begin

1 Choose WorkPlace

Make sure that you're signed on to AOL and click the **WorkPlace** button on the left side of the **Welcome** window. (You can also click the **Channels** icon in the toolbar and choose **WorkPlace**.) The **AOL WorkPlace** window opens.

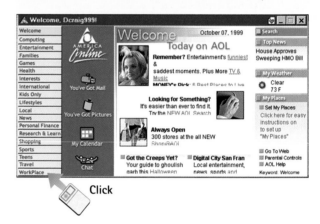

Click

2 Choose Start-Up Businesses

Click **Start-Up Businesses**. The **Start-Up Business** window opens.

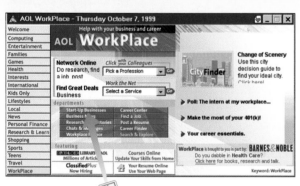

Click

3 Choose Getting Started

Click **Getting Started**. The **Getting Started** window opens.

Click

4 Choose Starting Your Business

This window is full of links to ideas and tools for helping you get started in business. In the list box, double-click **Starting Your Business-CCH**; you'll have to scroll down to find it. (If this article is not available or you see another that interests you, choose that one instead.) Note that double-clicking a topic that has a document icon to its left (it looks like a piece of paper with a fold in the upper-right corner) leads to an article that you can read. Double-clicking a topic that has a folder icon to its left displays another list of topics; keep opening folders until you find articles to read.

Double-click

6 Read the Article

Use the scrollbars to read the article. This is a hypertext document; clicking a bold underlined link takes you to a new page with information on the selected item. Use the buttons at the top left of this window to navigate between documents.

5 Choose the Right Small Business

The **Starting Your Business** window opens. Scroll down until you see **The right small business for you** link and double-click it to open the article. (Again, feel free to choose a different article that interests you.)

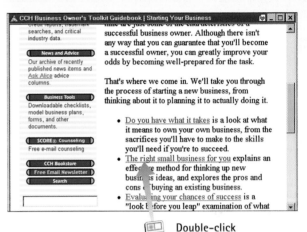

Double-click

How-To Hints

Explore the Starting Your Business Window

Take some time to investigate some of the other resources in the **Starting Your Business** window. Among other things, you can get credit reports, business plans, and business news and advice.

The Career Center

The **WorkPlace** channel is the gateway to an area called the **Career Center**. Use this area to find jobs, find out how to make more money in your job, write résumés, and more. Turn to the next task to learn more.

End

How to Use the Career Center

Maybe you're looking for a new job or help with your career. Or perhaps you want to find out about trends in the job market so that you can plan your education and future. The **Career Center** area offers a variety of services, including a database of job openings, career counseling, and even help with your résumé. If you try the **Career Center** at AOL, your next job may be only keystrokes away.

Begin

1 Choose WorkPlace

Make sure that you're signed on to AOL and click the **WorkPlace** button on the left side of the **Welcome** window. (You can also click the **Channels** icon in the toolbar and choose **WorkPlace**.) The **WorkPlace** window opens.

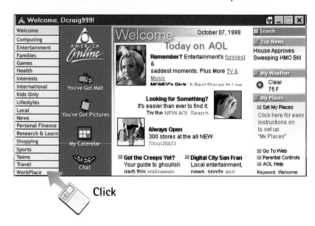

Click

2 Choose Career Center

Click **Career Center**. The **Career Center** window opens.

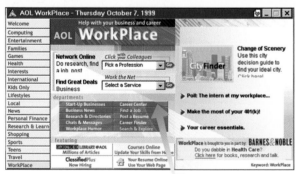

Click

3 Choose Gonyea Online Career Center

Click **Gonyea Online Career Center**. The **Gonyea Online Career Center** window opens.

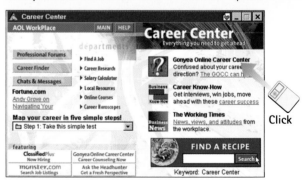

Click

4 Choose Job Hunting

Click **Job Hunting**. (If you want to explore a different area, such as **Career Counseling**, you can do that from this window, too.)

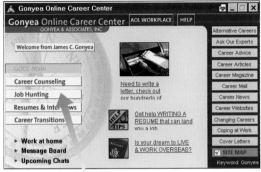

Click

5 Find a Job Hunting Topic

In the **Job Hunting** window, search for a topic that interests you and double-click it. As before, double-clicking a topic that has a document icon to its left leads to an article; double-clicking a topic that has a folder icon to its left displays another list of topics.

Double-click

6 Read the Article

Read the information you've found, scrolling as necessary.

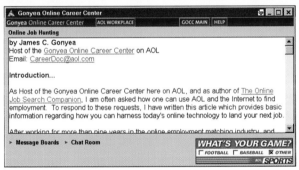

End

How-To Hints

For More Career Information

For information and job listings, click **ClassifiedPlus** in the **Career Center** window shown in Step 3. From this window, you can also consult other career topics, which provide information about career research and taking online courses, among other things.

Professional Forums

If you're looking for information on a particular career area, it's a good idea to investigate the professional forums, where you can find information about everything from accounting to marine biology to photography. (To get there, click **Professional Forums** in the initial **Career Center** window.) Not only can you hunt for jobs here, you can also keep up on what's going on in your field.

How to Use Reference Resources

AOL's **Research & Learn** channel provides you with reference resources such as encyclopedias, dictionaries, and phone books to help you find the information you need. In addition, the **Research & Learn** channel gives you access to libraries, statistics, quotes of the day, and more. In this task, you learn how to use the Merriam Webster online dictionary—just one of the many features available in this area.

Begin

1 Choose Research & Learn, Dictionary

Make sure that you're signed on to AOL and click the **Research & Learn** button on the left side of the **Welcome** window. (You can also click the **Channels** icon in the toolbar and choose **Research & Learn**.) The **AOL Research & Learn** window opens. Click **Dictionary** in the **References** section of this window.

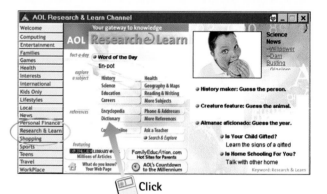

Click

2 Do a Single Word Search

The dictionary provides two ways to look up a word: single-word search and full-text search. Performing a single-word search is much like looking up words in a regular dictionary. You type the word in the upper text box and click **Look Up** to get a list of definitions.

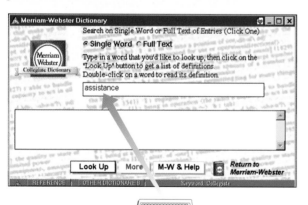

3 Review the Entries

The lower text box displays matching entries. Double-click a word to view its definition (Step 6 shows the window that displays the definition).

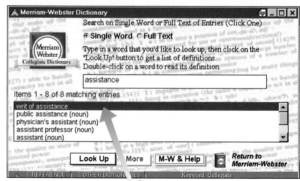

 Double-click

4 Do a Full Text Search

Change your search to full text by selecting the **Full Text** radio button. This type of search looks for words whose *definitions* contain the specified word. Click **Look Up**.

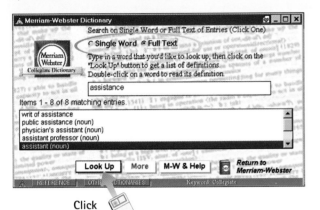

Click

5 Double-Click a Word

Notice that the matches for the full-text search are different than those for the single-word search. Double-click a word to view its definition.

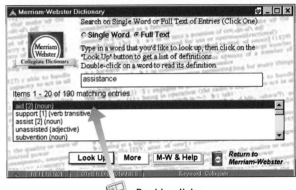

Double-click

6 Read the Definition

In the definition window for the selected word, scroll as necessary to read the text.

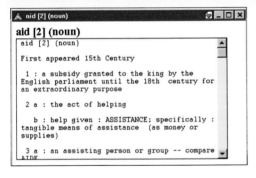

End

How-To Hints

Encyclopedias

In addition to providing a dictionary, AOL supplies a number of encyclopedias. To get to one, go to the main **Research & Learn** window (see Step 1) and click **Encyclopedia** in the **References** section.

Using a Different Dictionary

To use a different dictionary, click **Other Dictionaries** at the bottom of the **Dictionary** window. A long list of specialized dictionaries appears, including a computer and Internet dictionary, a birdwatcher's dictionary, and more.

How to Get Help for Teachers

AOL's **Research & Learn** channel provides many areas where teachers can gather and exchange information. This area is packed with resources, education libraries, forums, and information on professional organizations. Teachers from all disciplines will find information on lesson plans, grants, curriculum ideas, assessment, and technology in the classroom. In addition, there are opportunities to get your students involved in interactive, global learning activities. There's even an online university where you can take live classes. In this task, you learn about one part of the **Research & Learn** channel: the Electronic Schoolhouse. (You may also see this area referred to as the *Educator's Forum*.)

Begin

1 Choose Research & Learn, Education

Make sure that you're signed on to AOL and click the **Research & Learn** button on the left side of the **Welcome** window. In the **Research & Learn** window that opens, click **Education**. The **Education** window opens.

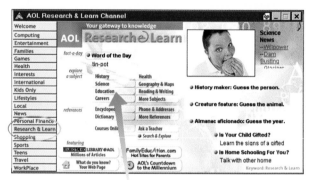

Click

2 Choose Resources for Educators

This window contains a list box displaying available education resources. Double-click **Resources for Educators**. The **Resources for Educators** window opens.

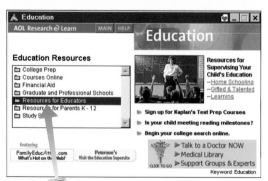

Double-click

3 Choose Electronic Schoolhouse

Double-click **Electronic Schoolhouse**. The **Educator's Forum** window opens.

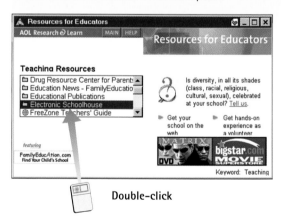

Double-click

4 Choose Project Libraries

Click **Project Libraries**. (Also notice that there are several message boards and links to Web pages in the list box.) The **Education Forum Download Libraries** window opens.

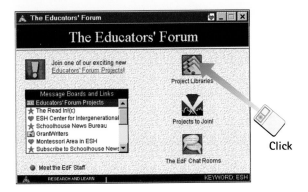

Click

5 Choose a Project Library

The project libraries are divided into areas. Select an area that interests you and click **Open**. The library window for your selection opens.

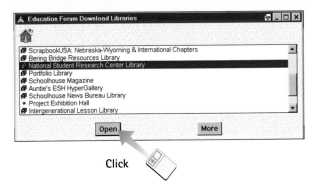

Click

6 Browse the Library

Select an item and click **Read Description** to find information on that item. If you want to download an item, click **Download Now** or **Download Later** (refer to Part 2 for more information on downloading).

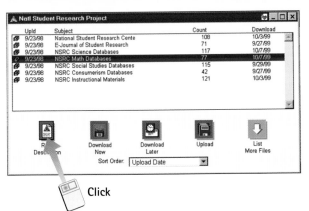

Click

End

How-To Hints

Chat with Teachers

The Electronic Schoolhouse also has a chat room where teachers can meet to hold discussions with fellow teachers. To get there, click **The EdF Chat Rooms** button on the right side of the **Educator's Forum** window.

Subscribing to the Schoolhouse Newsletter

From the list box in the **Educator's Forum** window, select **Subscribe to Schoolhouse News** to receive an electronic newsletter about the Electronic Schoolhouse.

How to Use the Software Center

If you're confused about all the software libraries online and how to use them, the **Software Center** is a great place to start. This area was created to give you an idea of just what types of utilities and applications are available in the computing forums. Visit the **Software Center** to discover programs you never even knew you needed.

Begin

1 Choose Computing

Make sure that you're signed on to AOL and click the **Computing** button on the left side of the **Welcome** window. (You can also click the **Channels** icon in the toolbar and choose **Computing**.) The **AOL Computing** window opens.

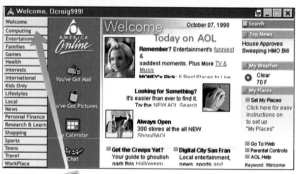

Click

2 Choose Download Software

Click **Download Center**. The **Download Center** window opens.

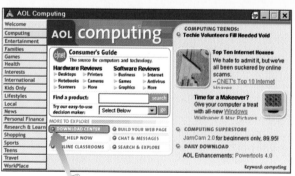

Click

3 Choose Education & Reference

The **Download Center** gives you an idea of software (both commercial and shareware) available for downloading. The most popular files are listed by category to make them easy to find. Make sure that the **Shareware** tab is selected and then double-click **Education & Reference**. The **Education & Reference** window opens.

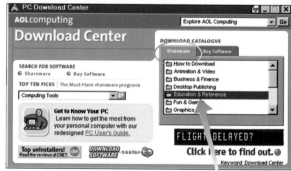

Double-click

4 Choose a Software Category

Double-click a category of software (such as **Science**) in the list box on the left side of this window.

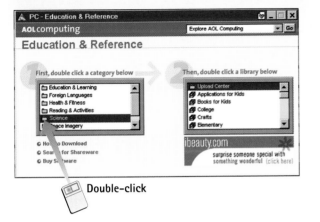

Double-click

5 Choose a Software Library

The list box on the right now lists software libraries for the category you selected in the left list box. To experiment, double-click the **Astronomy & Space** library.

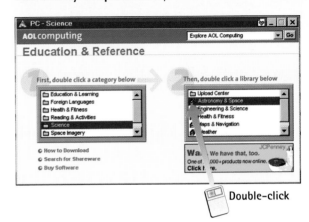

Double-click

6 Review the Available Software

The **Astronomy** window opens, listing astronomy-related software. If you want to read about any particular program, select it and click **Read Description**. If you need help downloading files, refer to Part 2.

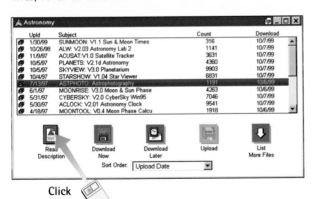

Click

End

How-To Hints

The Top Ten

For a list of the top ten shareware programs in a particular category, go to the **Download Center** window (shown in Step 3), choose a category from the **Top Ten Picks** drop-down list box, and click **Go**. A window displays the ten selected programs. Double-click a program name to open a window describing the program. You can download the program from here.

Uploading Files

There's also an **Upload** area in each category so that you can share your favorite software with others. Review the help files in each upload area for tips on sharing your files with other AOL members.

How to Research Health Topics

Perhaps one of the most interesting and useful topics you can research on AOL is health. Are you concerned about a particular health problem you or a family member is having? Or are you just curious about how to stay in the best possible shape, even though you currently don't have any health problems? Either way, dive into AOL's **Health** channel; you're sure to find some information appropriate for you.

Begin

1 Choose Health

Make sure that you're signed on to AOL and click the **Health** button on the left side of the **Welcome** window. (You can also click the **Channels** icon in the toolbar and choose **Health**.) The **AOL Health** window opens.

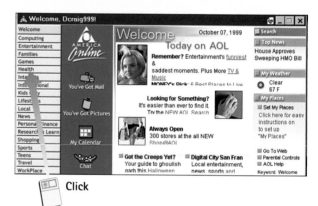

Click

2 Choose a Category

Choose a category of health-related information you want to explore. If you're interested in nontraditional medicine, for example, click **Alternative Medicine**. If you're searching for information on a specific medical problem, you can start by clicking **Conditions & Treatments**. (You can also look up illnesses directly by typing the illness name in the **Search** text box at top of the **AOL Health** window and clicking **Search**.)

Click

3 Choose an Illness Category

In the **Conditions & Treatments** window, choose an illness category. For example, if you are searching for information about osteoporosis, a bone disease, double-click **Bones, Joints, & Muscles**. (If your topic doesn't fall under the letters *A* through *C*, you must first click the tab for the appropriate letter of the alphabet.)

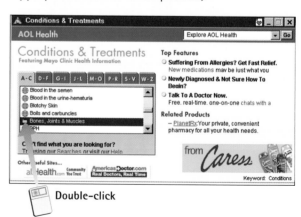

Double-click

4 Choose an Illness

From the list of illnesses that appears, select a specific illness. In the **Bones, Joints, & Muscles** window, for example, double-click **Osteoporosis**. A window full of information on the chosen topic opens.

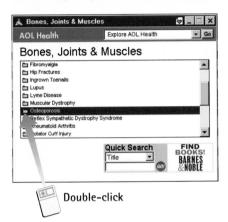

Double-click

5 Get an Overview

The overview window for the disease or condition is displayed by default. Read through this text to get a bird's-eye view of the subject. Under the word **Overview** is a series of other headings—such as **Risk Factors**, **Causes**, and **Complications**—that you can click to inform yourself further.

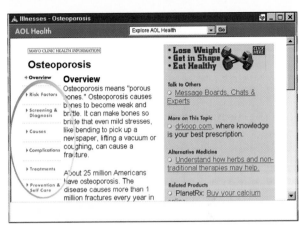

6 Follow Links

On the right side of the window are a series of links you can follow to gather additional information on the subject. For example, you can jump to chat rooms or message boards that discuss the disease you're interested in, or you can jump to other relevant Web sites, such as the National Osteoporosis Foundation.

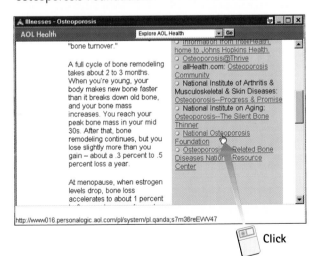

Click

End

How-To Hints

Looking Up Illnesses by Age or Sex

In addition to looking up illnesses in the **Conditions & Treatments** window, you can look them up by the age or sex group that tends to be afflicted. For example, you can look up osteoporosis under the category **Seniors**, which appears at the bottom of the initial **AOL Health** window.

Doing Your Own Research

AOL provides a medical reference department that enables you to carry out some of your own research. Among other things, you can consult medical databases and get in contact with health organizations. You can even hunt for a doctor online by using the **Doctor Finder**.

Task

Travel and Entertainment Channels

*B*ecause "travel" and "entertainment" mean different things to different people, AOL has several channels designed for your pleasure. The **Travel**, **Local**, and **International** channels will help you plan a trip—from the itinerary to the budget to the tickets. These channels can even take you on a virtual tour of local cities and international locations.

On the other hand, if traveling is not your idea of fun, you'll find an extensive selection of hobbies, shopping centers, sporting events, music, movies, fashion, and more in the **Interests**, **Entertainment**, **Shopping**, **Sports**, and **Computing** channels. ●

How to Plan Your Vacation

Either for business or pleasure, you can travel any-time—electronically, that is. Whether you're an actu-al traveler with reservations to make or an armchair traveler who wants to see some sunshine on a drab winter day, AOL's **Travel** channel is the place to be. The **Travel** channel helps you choose a destination, plan an itinerary, draft a travel budget, and make all the necessary reservations. Wherever you're going— a business trip to Chicago, a family vacation to Hawaii, or a weekend getaway to Toronto—AOL can help you get there and enjoy yourself after you arrive.

Begin

1 Choose Destinations

Make sure that you're signed on to AOL. Click the **Travel** button on the left side of the **Welcome** window. (You can also click the **Channels** icon in the toolbar and choose **Travel**.) In the **AOL Travel** window, click **Destinations**. The **Destination Guides** window opens.

Click

2 Create a Miniguide

Click the **Fodor's** button to start creat-ing a custom miniguide. The **Create a Custom Miniguide** window opens.

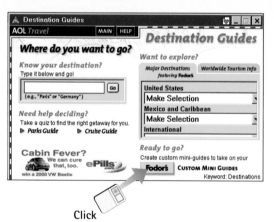

Click

3 Choose a Location

Your first step in creating a miniguide is to choose a location (such as Kauai) and click **Continue**. (You may have to scroll down to locate the **Continue** button.)

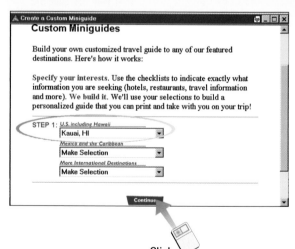

Click

4 Select Categories

Now choose the categories of information you want to include in your miniguide. Click **Continue** after you've made your selections.

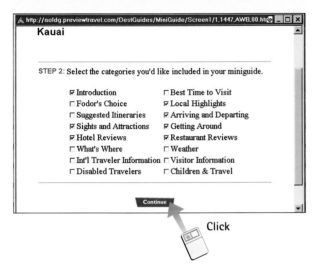

Click

5 Narrow Your Choices

In the next miniguide screen, you get a chance to be more specific about the choices you made in Step 4. For example, if you chose to view information about hotels, you can now choose what physical area you want to look in and what price range you'll consider. Make your selections and click **Continue**. (The more check boxes you selected in the preceding step, the more choices you'll have to make here.)

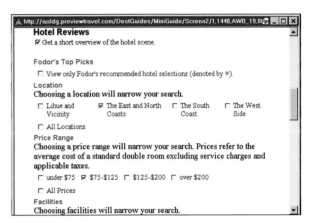

6 Read Your Miniguide

Your custom miniguide will be generated. Now you can read it at your leisure, or print it out so that you can take it with you on your travels.

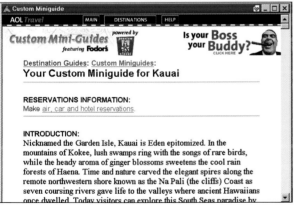

End

How-To Hints

Make Your Reservations

After you've decided on a final location, return to the **AOL Travel** window (shown in Step 1) and click **Reservations** to go to the **Reservations Center**. From there, you can make plane, hotel, and car reservations, among other things.

Going Directly There

You can also look up travel destinations by entering their names in the list box in the initial **Destinations Guides** window (shown in Step 2) and clicking **Go**.

How to Find Out About Your Local Area

Local is AOL's channel for U.S. cities that have joined the information age. You can find all kinds of information—maybe even about your hometown—on AOL. Use the **Local** channel to find weather, news, community information, and even the political lowdown on a city you'd like to visit. Or check out your hometown for entertainment, sport schedules, restaurants, the lottery, and maybe some special features you weren't even aware of. The **Local** channel makes it easy to tour U.S. cities online.

Begin

1 Choose Local

Make sure that you're signed on to **AOL**. Click the **Local** button on the left side of the **Welcome** window. (You can also click the **Channels** icon in the toolbar and choose **Local**.) The **Digital City** window opens.

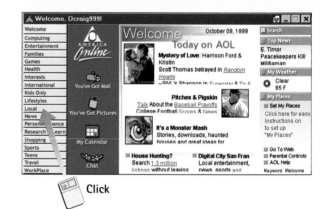

Click

2 Choose Local News

This window displays a map of the United States. You can access Digital City information by clicking a location on the map or by selecting a category. For this example, click the **Local News** category. The **News & Issues** window opens.

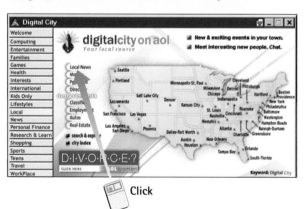

Click

3 Choose a City

In the **Select a City** area, click a city you're interested in (for this example, I clicked **Albuquerque - Santa Fe**; of course, you can click any other city that strikes your fancy).

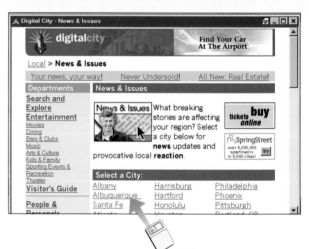

Click

4 Read Local News

You'll see a window with information specific to the selected area. On the right side of the window is a news article of local interest. Scroll down to read through this article.

5 Choose Links

For instant access to movies, music, shopping, travel, and more in the area you've selected, click the appropriate link on the left side of the window. (The links available depend somewhat on the location.)

End

How-To Hints

Buying, Selling, or Renting?

Are you looking for a place to rent or buy? Explore the Real Estate department by clicking **Real Estate** from the initial **Digital City** window (shown in Step 2).

Check Out the Classified Ads

If you're moving to a new spot, you might be hunting for a job, an apartment, a car, and some new furniture all at once. In this case—or even if you're not moving anywhere but are searching for any one of those things—you can start by consulting Digital City's classi-fied ads. Just click **Classifieds** in the initial **Digital City** window.

Using the Visitor's Guide

Another way to find out about a wide range of local happenings is to use the **Visitor's Guide**, available from the News & Issues window you saw in Step 3. From here, you can find scads of information on local attractions, hotels, museums, and much more.

How to Take an International Voyage

The **International** channel can transport you to the far corners of the world. Dozens of countries worldwide have information and Web sites in this area. Meet with other travelers and share ideas about the countries you've explored or have always wanted to visit. While you're traveling abroad, brush up on your language skills at the **Bistro**, where you can discuss a variety of topics in languages from Spanish to Arabic to Chinese to Tagalog. Whether you've traveled the world or have never left your hometown, the **International** channel is always an exciting vacation.

Begin

1 Choose International

Make sure that you're signed on to AOL and click the **International** button on the left side of the **Welcome** window. (You can also click the **Channels** icon in the toolbar and choose **International**.) The AOL International Channel window opens.

Click

2 Choose a Continent

This window includes a map that enables you to access information about various continents. To experiment, click **Australia** in the map. The **Australia & Oceania** window opens.

Click

3 Choose a Country

The list box on the left side of the window lists the specific countries in the area you've selected. Double-click the country you want to know more about. For this example, double-click **Australia** to open the **Australia** window.

 Double-click

4 Choose a Topic

To find out more about this country, scroll through the list box and double-click a topic that appeals to you. To experiment, double-click **Travel & Culture**. In the **Travel & Culture** window, double-click **Lonely Planet's Australia**. (The Lonely Planet Press puts out a series of highly regarded travel guides.)

Double-click

5 Continue Exploring

The Lonely Planet guide provides a fascinating overview of the country, its land, and its culture. Click an additional link to learn more about that aspect of the country. Here, I clicked the **Off the Beaten Track** link.

Click

6 View Additional Sites

If this doesn't make you want to immediately pack your bags for Australia, it's not clear what will! You can double-click any of the other locations to read all about them.

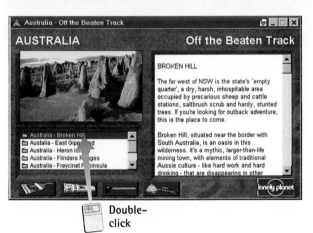

Double-click

End

How-To Hints

Hunting for Countries

If you're not sure how to locate the country you want using the map shown in Step 2, click **Country Information** from the main **AOL International Channel** window. From the next window, you can choose a continent and then search for a country within it.

Chatting Internationally

Click **Global Meeting Place** in the initial **International Channel** window to find an area where you can communicate with other members. You can also access the **Bistro** from this area. Currently, the **Bistro** has chat sessions available for more than a dozen languages—from Hindi to Japanese to Russian.

How to Find Recipes

If you're looking for a place to meet people with common interests, or if you have a hobby you want more information on, visit AOL's **Interests** channel. This channel provides information about automobiles, pets, home and garden, and much more. Each area provides its own collections of information, message boards, searchable databases, chat rooms, and Web connections. In this task, you'll find out how to look up recipes in the **Food & Recipes** area (everyone has to eat). This area may come in handy whether you're looking for fresh ideas for a special holiday dinner or just trying to whip together a quick summer picnic.

Begin

1 Choose Interests

Make sure that you're signed on to AOL and click the **Interests** button on the left side of the **Welcome** window. (You can also click the **Channels** icon in the toolbar and choose **Interests**.) The AOL **Interests** window opens.

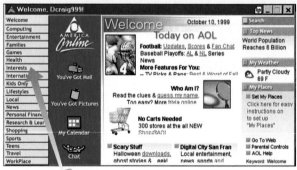

Click

2 Choose Food & Recipes

Look through the available topics. For this task, click **Food & Recipes**. The **Food & Recipes** window opens.

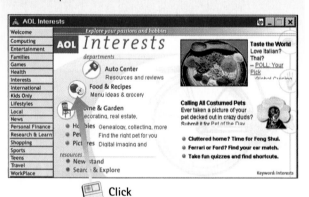

Click

3 Enter an Ingredient

In the **Recipe Finder** text box, type the name of an ingredient you want to search for. To experiment, type **chocolate** and click the **Search** button.

4 View the Search Results

You'll see a search results window such as this one. Browse through the window to see whether you turned up anything that catches your fancy.

5 Look at More Recipes

If you entered a fairly general search category, such as **chocolate**, you may have turned up a fair number of recipes. (My search turned up more than 1,000!) To travel to other pages of recipes, click the navigation buttons at the bottom of the window. Clicking **Next Page** takes you to the next page; clicking **Previous Page** takes you to the previous page (this option becomes available if you're not on the first page). You can also click a number to go to a specific page.

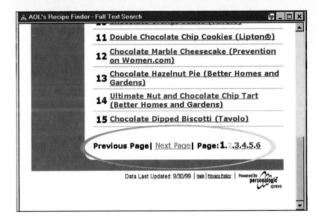

6 Choose a Recipe

When you find a recipe that grabs your interest, click it to select it. A recipe window will open. If it seems like the right choice, you'll probably want to print it (see the How-To Hints for details). If not, you can continue to browse through the recipes you've turned up to see whether something else is more appealing.

How-To Hints

Printing Recipes

To print a recipe, first click the **Print** option that appears within the recipe window; it should say **view a printable page**. (Although you can print without clicking this button, you'll wind up with a lot of extra garbage on the page.) Then click the **Print** button in the AOL toolbar.

Going Out to Eat?

If you are tired of cooking and want to go out for a change, look into the **Local Dining Guide** (choose **Local Dining** from the **Food & Recipes** window and a city from the window that appears). If you live in or are traveling to a large-enough city, you may be able to scope out some interesting restaurants.

End

How to Get the Scoop on Pets

Some of us have pets that we consider members of the family. If you already have pets and are looking for information about pet health, training, and more, you can check out the pet area in the **Interests** channel. If you don't yet have pets but are in the market, you can also come here to learn which breeds might be right for you.

Begin

1 Choose Interests

Make sure that you're signed on to AOL and click the **Interests** button on the left side of the **Welcome** window. (You can also click the **Channels** icon in the toolbar and choose **Interests**.) The AOL **Interests** window opens.

Click

2 Choose Pets

Look through the topics available. For this task, click **Pets**. The **Pets** window opens.

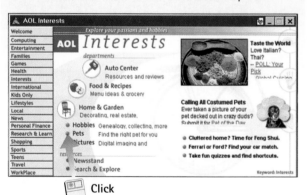

Click

3 Choose Dog Breed Overviews

Click **Dog Breed Overviews**. (Of course, if you're a cat person, you can click **Cat Breed Overviews** instead.)

Click

4 Choose Go to Breeds

In the **Best of Breeds** window that opens, click **Go to Breeds**.

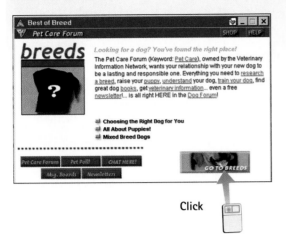

Click

5 Choose a Breed

In the resulting window, scroll until you find a breed that appeals to you. (You may be scrolling for a while; there are a lot of choices here!) Double-click your choice to open a window with information about that breed.

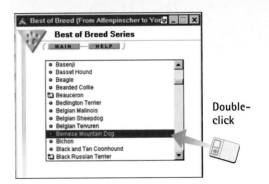

Double-click

6 Read about the Breed

Now you can read up on the breed you selected. From this window, you can also go to message boards about the selected breed or read through a catalog of books.

End

How-To Hints

Mixed Breed Dogs

Purebred dogs are not for everyone. It's not hard to find mixed breed dogs who are exceptionally loyal, handsome, and good tempered. You can also feel good about rescuing an animal from confinement to the animal shelter or worse. If you want to learn more about dogs of uncertain ethnic heritage, click the link **Mixed Breed Dogs** in the initial **Best of Breed** window (shown in Step 4).

Pet Rescue

Both mixed breed and purebred dogs far too often find themselves in need of rescuing. If you'd like more information about animal rescue, click **Pets Index** in the **Pets** window (shown in Step 3) and then click **Pet Rescue Clearinghouse**. You might be able to both find yourself the perfect companion and save an animal's life.

How to Scope Out the Latest Movies

If you're a movie fan, AOL is the place to be (at least until you're in a theater seat). You can look at the latest movies before you go to the theater, plus get sneak previews of the hottest new releases. You can download pictures of your favorite stars and talk about the movies in designated message boards and chat rooms. AOL members also have opportunities to receive great promotional items such as posters, movie passes, and more.

Begin

1 Choose Entertainment

Make sure that you're signed on to AOL and click the **Entertainment** button on the left side of the **Welcome** window. (You can also click the **Channels** icon in the toolbar and choose **Entertainment**.) The **AOL Entertainment** window opens.

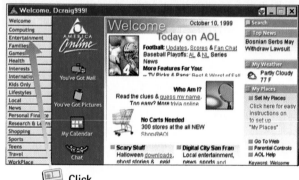

Click

2 Choose Movies

Look at the major areas listed at the top of the window. For this task, click **Movies**. The **Movies** window opens.

Click

3 Choose the Movies Index

If you see the movie you want to read about, click its link. Otherwise, click **movies: index**.

Click

4 Choose Entertainment Asylum: Movies

In the next window that appears, double-click **Entertainment Asylum: Movies**. (If you see another category that piques your interest, feel free to explore that one in addition to or instead of.) The **Entertainment Asylum Movies** window opens.

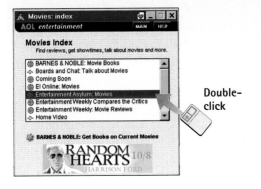

Double-click

5 Pick a Movie

Choose a movie you want to read about. You can either click to select the featured movie (in this example, the featured movie is **Random Hearts**), or you can double-click a movie in the alphabetical list under **More Movie Features**.

Click

6 Read about the Movie

A synopsis window opens; scroll through it to get a summary of the movie. From this window, you should also be able to jump to a picture gallery, participate in a poll, get tickets and show times, visit chat rooms, and more.

End

How-To Hints

Using the MovieFone

Do you like to know what movies are playing in your neighborhood, and where, and when? If so, the MovieFone is for you. To get there, click **MovieFone** in the initial **Movies** window (shown in Step 3). In the resulting **MovieFone** window, type your zip code and choose whether to search by theater, movie title, or a number of other categories. You also have the option of searching by city or by state.

What's Out on Video?

If you want to see a movie but are not in the mood to leave the house (or the couch, for that matter), check out what's available in video. From the initial **Movies** window, click the **Home Video** link and go exploring from there.

How to Enjoy Music on America Online

AOL's **Music** area is a great place for music lovers. You'll find your favorite artists in styles ranging from country to classical to rock to R&B and more. The latest tour dates, CD information, and industry happenings are all at your fingertips. You'll even find artist profiles, sound clips, and video clips. All in all, the **Music** area on AOL is the cool place to be.

Begin

1 Choose Entertainment

Make sure that you're signed on to AOL and click the **Entertainment** button on the left side of the **Welcome** window. (You can also click the **Channels** icon in the toolbar and choose **Entertainment**.) The **Entertainment** window opens.

Click

2 Choose Music

In the **Entertainment** window, click **Music**. The **Music** window opens.

Click

3 Choose a Music Category

This window is a wonderful resource for new releases and music information. To experiment, click **Classical**. (Obviously, if you can't tolerate classical music but love hip-hop or jazz, you should choose one of those categories instead.)

Click

4 Choose a Featured Release

In the **Classical** window that opens, click a featured release to find out more about it. (You can also read a more extensive article about a featured artist—in this case **Nadja Salerno-Sonnenberg**—if you like.)

 Click

5 Read about the Release

In the window that opens, you can read about the release. From this window, you may also be able to find out more about the artist or artists, about the record label, and, of course, about how to order the CD.

6 Hear, Review, or Buy a CD

If you return to the **Classical** window, you can listen to, review, or buy one of the featured CDs—just by clicking the **Hear It**, **Review It**, or **Buy It** button. The **Hear It** button lets you download a **.WAV** file you can play to hear a sample from the CD. The **Review It** button leads to message boards about the CD. The **Buy It** button takes you to a CDNOW window, from which you can purchase the CD in question, as well as search for and buy other CDs. (Buying should be as easy as possible, after all!)

End

How-To Hints

Finding Other CDs

To find CDs other than those that are featured, you can click on the **CDNOW** button (under the text **Buy Music on Sale @**). This link takes you to the CDNOW classical page (you'll see another page if you chose a different music category), from which you can search for CDs by composer, conductor, performer, album title and more. (The available choices depend on the music category you selected.)

Talk About Music

If you're in the mood to talk about music, click **Chat & Messages** in the initial **Music** window (shown in Step 3). You'll find a wealth of message boards and chat rooms on such diverse topics as Pavarotti, Madonna, and the Grateful Dead.

How to Shop Online

AOL offers so many online stores, it's impossible to show them all here. Instead, you'll experiment with a single store—one that should be of particular interest to chocolate lovers. Although each online store operates in its own unique way, this task gives you at least a taste of online shopping on AOL.

Begin

1 Choose Shopping

Make sure that you're signed on to AOL and click the **Shopping** button on the left side of the **Welcome** window. (You can also click the **Channels** icon in the toolbar and choose **Shopping**.) The **Shopping Main** window opens.

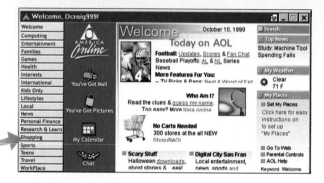

Click

2 Choose A–Z Listing of Stores

If you know what you're shopping for, you can click a product category, such as **Home & Garden** or **Computing**. If you know the name of the store you're looking for (as in this task), click **A–Z Listing of Stores**. The **Complete Store Listings** window opens; scroll until you see **Godiva Chocolatier** in the list box, and then click it. (If you have no particular fondness for chocolate, feel free to pick a different store.)

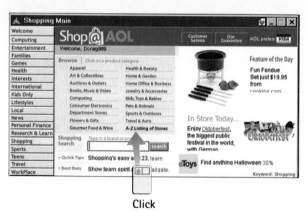

Click

3 Find the Item You Want

The **Godiva Chocolates** window opens. This store is divided into several different product categories, such as **Birthday Collection** and **Halloween Collection**. (These categories may change, depending on the season.) Click **U.S. Shop Online** and then click the chocolate collection you want to order—such as **All Occasion**. In the window that appears, click an item you'd like to order.

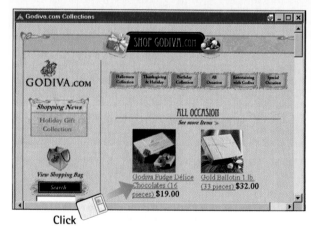

Click

4 Add to Your Shopping Bag

The resulting window describes the product in greater detail. If you like what you see, add the item to your "shopping bag" (the list of items you want to buy) by clicking **Add to Shopping Bag**. The **Shopping Bag** window appears so that you can see the item you ordered. (From this window, click **Return to Shopping** to add additional items to your shopping bag, if necessary.)

Click

5 Checking Out

When you've added all the desired items to your shopping bag, click the **Checkout** button in your **Shopping Bag** window. In the next several windows, supply the requested billing information, shipping information, and gift message, clicking **Continue** or **Next** in each window to move to the next one. In the order review window, check that everything looks okay and click **Next** to proceed.

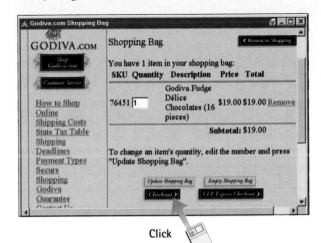

Click

6 Submit Your Order

Finally, and most importantly, enter your credit card information and click **Submit Order**.

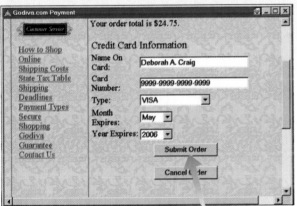

 Click

End

How-To Hints

How to Shop

Remember that shopping at other online stores might not be the same as shopping at the Godiva store. Some stores use an electronic shopping cart; others don't. Shopping in some stores is free; others charge membership fees. Be patient, read each store's instructions, and you'll soon be an online shopping expert.

Secure Shopping

Shopping on AOL is secure. AOL can't guarantee, however, that your transactions will be secure when you are shopping on the Web. Don't use your credit card or give out personal information at a Web site if you're not sure that the site is safe.

How to Check Baseball Standings

If you love sports, you probably like to know what the score was as well as the standings of your favorite team or athlete. AOL has all the information you need—online and up to date. Why worry about what time the news comes on (and whether they'll cover your team) or why the newspaper isn't on your doorstep? Connect to AOL whenever it's convenient for you, and check the standings in the AOL **Sports** channel.

Begin

1 Choose Sports

Make sure that you're signed on to AOL and click the **Sports** button on the left side of the **Welcome** window. (You can also click the **Channels** icon in the toolbar and choose **Sports**.) The AOL **Sports** window opens.

Click

2 Choose Baseball

This area is full of sports information, scores, news, and areas for fans to play games, enter contests, and meet other fans. Click **Baseball**. (If it's not baseball season, baseball standings won't be available, in which case you can check the standings for some other sport.)

Click

3 Choose Standings

On the right side of the **Baseball** window, click the **Standings** tab.

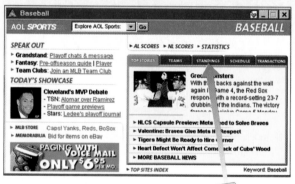

Click

4 Choose Expanded MLB Standings

From the list in the **Standings** tab, click **Expanded MLB Standings**. An **MLB Standings** window opens.

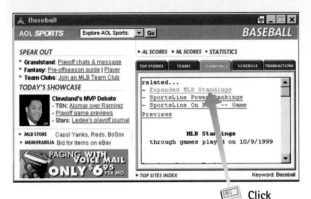

Click

5 Choose Expanded MLB Standings

Scroll through this window to see the standings for teams in both leagues.

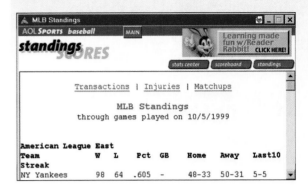

6 Check Out the Stats

If you want stats, AOL has stats. Click the **Stats Center** button in the **MLB Standings** window to go to the **MLB Statistics Center** window. From this window, you can get statistics on everything from pitching to hitting to team stats to the stats for individual players.

End

How-To Hints

Investigating the Sports Channel

The **Sports** channel covers everything from football to tennis to golf and more. To find out more, go exploring in the main **AOL Sports** window. You can also check out the **Grandstand** area (click **Talk About It** in the main AOL **Sports** window) for chat areas, message boards, software libraries, and more.

Using Search & Explore

Click the **Search** button on the main **AOL Sports** window to help locate specific sports information.

How to Meet Like Minds

AOL has literally millions of members, so some of them are bound to share not only your interests, but also your outlook and philosophy of life. The **Lifestyles** channel is where you can meet and interact with these people. In this area, you can find people of the same age, religion, ethnicity, sexual orientation, and more. In this task, you'll inform yourself about the American Association of Retired Persons—an important group representing older citizens.

Begin

1 Choose Lifestyles

Make sure that you're signed on to AOL and click the **Lifestyles** button on the left side of the **Welcome** window. (You can also click the **Channels** icon in the toolbar and choose **Lifestyles**.) The **Lifestyles** window opens.

Click

2 Choose a Department

Click **Ages & Stages**. (If another area strikes your fancy—suppose that you're a teenager or you're interested in self improvement—feel free to check out that department instead.)

Click

3 Choose Ages & Stages

In the **Ages & Stages** window, click **Ages & Stages Communities**. (A number of the departments have similar "communities" links representing groups of people with a common interest or connection.) The **Ages & Stages Communities** window opens.

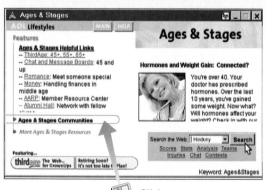

Click

4 Choose AARP

Under **Ages & Stages Communities**, choose a "community"—in this case, the communities are based on age groups. For this example, double-click **AARP** (the American Association of Retired Persons). If you're on the opposite end of the age spectrum or if another category appeals to you more, investigate that one instead.

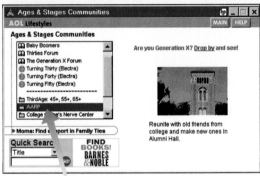

Double-click

5 Choose Boards

The **AARP Online** window opens. Click **Boards** to go to a window listing available AARP bulletin boards. (If you like, you can click **Chat** to check out the times and subjects of AARP chat rooms, or you can click **Contact Us** to find out about what AARP is, what some of the benefits of membership are, and how to contact the organization.)

Click

6 Check Out the AARP Bulletin

In the resulting window, you can scope out the bulletin boards. When you find a topic that interests you, double-click it to learn more about the subject.

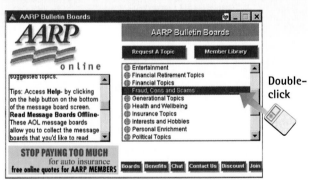
Double-click

End

How-To Hints

Choose the Right Department

The **Lifestyles** channel includes everything from the wacky to the sublime. In your travels, you may wind up in a department that strikes you as silly or even uncomfortable. (Maybe you've landed in numerology when you were hoping to read up on Judaism; or maybe you wound up in romance when you meant to delve into family issues.) In this case, instead of getting bent out of shape, it's best to backtrack until you find a topic or department that's more up your alley.

Get Your Bearings

Like many of the other channels, the **Lifestyles** channel includes a **Search & Explore** feature. This is a great place to start if you want to get your bearings in the channel.

Task

Kids and the Family

AOL is a family-oriented service provider. AOL's **Families**, **Kids Only**, and **Teens** channels offer dozens of educational and entertainment opportunities suitable for young people and fun for adults. The tasks in this part introduce a few of these features. First, you'll learn how to get help with your homework. (Not surprisingly, this is one of AOL's most popular features.) Then, you'll discover how you can find fun and functional software—and software assistance—to use at home. You'll also stop by the Web and see the **Kids AOL NetFind** area for searching **Kids Only** sites on the Internet. Then you'll learn how to carry out some genealogical research to track down the roots of your family. Finally, you'll tour the **Games** area and join a game of Slingo. ●

How to Get Homework Help

Homework can be a real chore. Sometimes the assignment seems boring; other times it's hard to understand. You could ask your parents for help, but they don't always know the answers. Besides, they might be busy. So who else can you ask for help? Well, who better to help you with homework than a teacher? Using AOL's **Homework Help** message boards, you can ask a teacher questions and get responses soon thereafter. Whether the subject is arithmetic or astronomy, zoology or Zagreb, one of AOL's knowledgeable online teachers can guide you toward solving all your homework problems.

Begin

1 Choose Kids Only

Make sure that you're signed on to AOL and click the **Kids Only** button on the left side of the **Welcome** window. (You can also click the **Channels** icon in the toolbar and choose **Kids Only**.) The **AOL Kids Only** window opens.

Click

2 Choose Homework Help

This area is packed with information and activities especially for kids. For this task, you want help with your homework, so click **Homework Help**. The **Homework Help** window opens.

Click

3 Choose Ask a Teacher

Click **Ask a Teacher**. The **Kids Only Homework Help** message board window appears.

Click

4 Choose a General Category

This window displays a list of categories of homework help message boards. Double-click the category you want help with, such as **Math** or **Social Studies**.

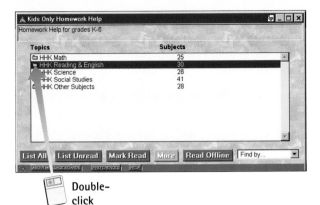

Double-click

5 Choose a More Specific Topic

In the next window that appears, look again for a topic that interests you and double-click it.

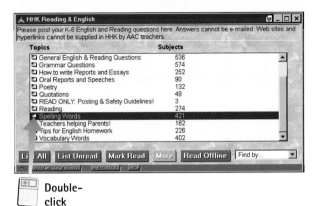

Double-click

6 Create a Posting

From the next window, you can read the various postings (double-click to open them) to get a feel for the discussion on this message board. If you want to post a question of your own, click the **Create Subject** button. In the **Post New Message** window that appears, type a subject and then type your question. (*Make sure that your subject line is informative.* It's harder to find the response to the question `I need help!!!` than `Need help with report on quarks`.) When you're done, click **Send**. Revisit the message board later that day or the next day; most likely someone will have posted a response to your question.

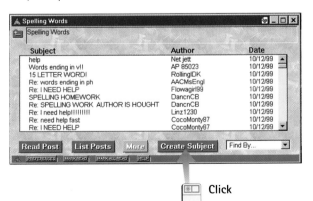

Click

How-To Hints

Looking Up Stuff

The **Homework Help** window (shown in Step 3) includes buttons for accessing an online dictionary, encyclopedia, thesaurus, and knowledge base (the knowledge base is full of answers to the questions asked most often in the tutoring areas).

Other Ways of Getting Help

Another helpful alternative is the tutoring room (click **Tutoring Room** from the **Homework Help** window). When these chat rooms are open, you can use them to get one-on-one tutoring on math, science, and more. (Unfortunately, if you're on a **Kids Only** account and Instant Messages are turned off, you won't be able to receive tutoring.) Another way to get homework help is to visit the **Ask a Teacher** area (you can get there through the **Research & Learn** channel). From here, people of all ages—not just kids—can get help with their homework.

End

How to Find Software in the Kids Only Channel

AOL knows that everyone has different interests in computer software and information, so it has created software libraries just for kids. In these libraries, you can find information about computers and educational software. The **Kids Only** software libraries also include games, puzzles, and guides for writing and programming. If you hunt long enough, you're sure to find something that's fun, interesting, or both!

Begin

1 Choose Kids Only

Make sure that you're signed on to AOL and click the **Kids Only** button on the left side of the **Welcome** window. (You can also click the **Channels** icon in the toolbar and choose **Kids Only**.) The AOL Kids Only window opens.

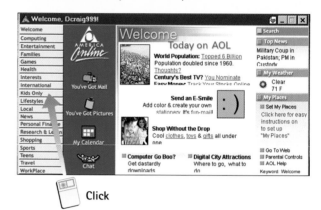

Click

2 Choose Games

There are software libraries in many parts of the **Kids Only** area. For this task, click **Games** to check out what's there. The **Kids Only Games** window opens.

Click

3 Choose Download Games

This window has links to seasonal and thematic games as well as help for playing electronic games. To download games you can play while you're offline, click the **Download Games** button. The **Games Download** window opens.

Click

4 Choose a Game

Scroll through the text box to find a game title that interests you. When you find a likely candidate, double-click it.

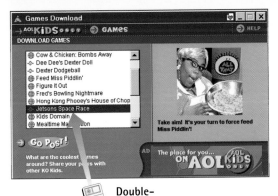

Double-click

5 Read About the Game

You'll see a window describing the selected game. Read about the game to find out whether you're interested enough to try it out. If you decide to try the game, click **For PC** or **For Mac**, depending on the type of computer you have. (If you decide not to download the game, return to the **Games Download** window and make another selection.)

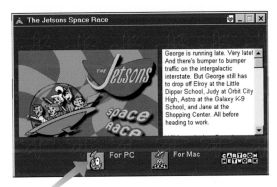

Click

6 Download the Game

In the window that appears, carefully note how big the file is and how long it will take to download. Also check for any required equipment or software. If you decide to go ahead with the download, click **Download Now**. (You can also click **Download Later** to download the file during an Automatic AOL session; if necessary, go back to Part 2, "America Online Features," to refresh your memory on how to schedule Automatic AOL sessions.)

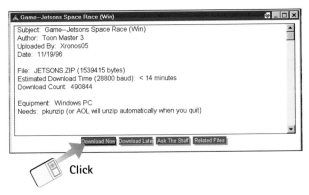

Click

End

How-To Hints

Find Out More About Downloading

Refer to Task 5, "How to Use the Download Manager," in Part 2 if you need help downloading files.

More Games

To check out more games, you can click one of the top games listed in the initial **Kids Only Games** window. These games change frequently, but you might see ones such as **Haunted Alphabet** or **Dreamcast Central**. In addition, you can go to the **Games Download** window (shown in Step 4), double-click the **PC Downloads** folder in the list box, choose a category of games (such as **Arcade Games** or **Card Games**), and browse through the games in the selected category until you find one that interests you. What's more, AOL provides a number of online games; to get to these, just click the **Online Games** link in the **Kids Only Games** window.

How to Use AOL NetFind for Kids

Finding stuff on the Internet can be hard. AOL's **NetFind for Kids** area is specially designed to find the kind of Web sites kids want to visit. If you have to write a paper for class, just type your topic in the search box and click **Find**. AOL's NetFind will return a list of sites with the information you need to start your research. When school is out and you have time to have fun, use the **AOL NetFind for Kids** page to search for games and puzzles or your favorite hobby. **NetFind for Kids** searches through Web sites designed with kids in mind—which makes the Internet a fun, safe place to play and learn.

Begin

1 Choose Kids Only

Make sure that you're signed on to AOL and click the **Kids Only** button on the left side of the **Welcome** window. (You can also click the **Channels** toolbar icon and choose **Kids Only**.) The **AOL Kids Only** window opens.

Click

2 Choose AOL NetFind

Click **AOL NetFind**. You'll see the AOL NetFind Kids Only page.

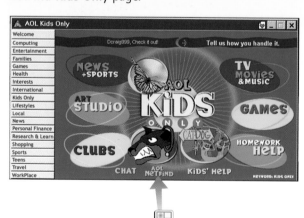

Click

3 Start a Search

This page not only helps you search for words on the Internet, it also has links to lots of interesting pages. Scroll through the page to see what's available. When you're ready to start searching, type your search word in the text box and click **Find**.

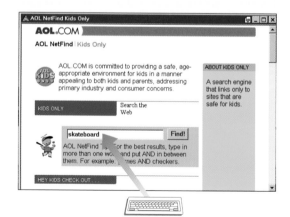

4 View the Search Results

The AOL NetFind tool soon returns a list of sites that match your search word. Scroll through the list of sites to see if anything seems interesting.

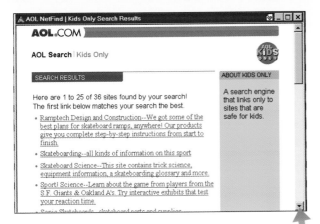

Click

5 View More Sites

If you've scrolled all the way to the bottom of the list and haven't found what you're looking for, click **More Sites**.

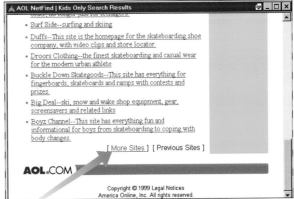

Click

6 Go to a Site

A new page of search results appears. After you've found a site you'd like to look at, click the item (it's a link) to go there. (If you want to go back to the sites you saw initially, click the **Previous Sites** button.)

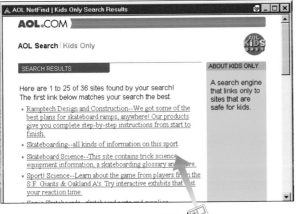

Click

End

How-To Hints

Refining Your Search

If you can't find what you are looking for, try using multiple words in your search, separated by the word **and**. For example, if you want to find information on mountain bicycles, try typing **mountain and bicycles** in the search box. This should find Web sites that match *both* search words. (If you type **mountain bicycles** instead, NetFind tracks down all sites that contain *either* search word.)

You can also use the word **or** in your searches. The string **bicycles or rollerblades** finds sites about bicycling *and* sites about rollerblading.

Another option is to search using the word **not**. Searching for **skates not rollerblades** produces a list of Web sites that are about skating *but not about* rollerblading.

How to Trace Your Genealogy

Many of us are fascinated with our family histories—whether it's determining who's who in Aunt Evelyn's family album, or trying to pin down the fine points of who immigrated to the United States and when. Regardless of your ancestry, AOL is a great place to start tracing your genealogy.

Begin

1 Choose Families

Make sure that you're signed on to AOL and click the **Families** button on the left side of the **Welcome** window. (You can also click the **Channels** icon in the toolbar and choose **Families.**) The **AOL Families Channel** window opens.

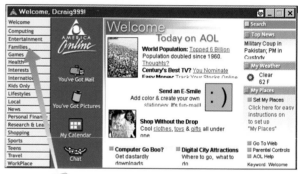

Click

2 Choose Family Life & Genealogy

This window offers links to all kinds of family-related topics. To explore the genealogy link, click **Family Life & Genealogy.**

Click

3 Choose the Genealogy Tab

In the resulting **Family Life and Genealogy** window, click the **Genealogy** tab.

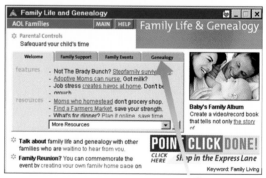

Click

4 Choose the Library of Congress

From the **Genealogy** tab, click the link that takes you to the Library of Congress. This is a world-renowned source of genealogical material.

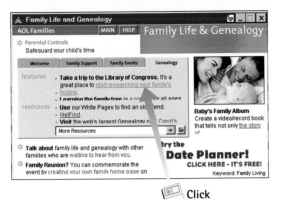

Click

5 Browse the Library

Browse through this Library of Congress page to get an idea of what's available. There's a lot here! Among other things, you'll find resources on African American genealogy, English genealogy, Welsh genealogy, and much more. There's also an invaluable list of other genealogical resources on the Web.

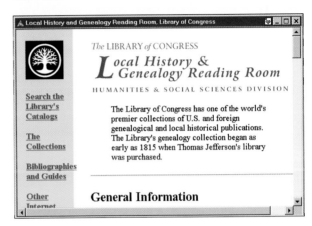

6 Choose a Source

When you find a genealogical source that interests you, click it. Most likely, you'll reach a page that is literally crammed full of references to other materials on the selected area of genealogy. Have fun in your research!

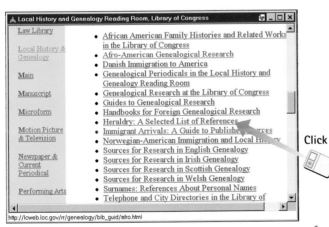

Click

End

How-To Hints

Explore More Genealogical Resources

In the **Family Life and Genealogy** window, check out the drop-down list at the bottom of the **Genealogy** tab (it lists **More Resources** as the default) for an extensive list of online locations—other than the Library of Congress—that are useful for researching genealogy. (**Cyndi's List of Genealogy Sites** is a good place to start.) Select the desired resource from the drop-down list and click **Go**.

Genealogical Chat

If you're fascinated with genealogy, you may want to chat about it with others of like mind. To do so, click the chat link under the **Genealogy** tab in the **Family Life and Genealogy** window. In the **About Family Life** window that comes up, check out the **Genealogy Forum**.

5

How to Play Slingo

Kids and adults need more than school and work; they need to have fun. With this in mind, AOL offers dozens of different games you can play online: action, sports, role playing, classic, simulation, and strategy—every kind of game you can imagine is in AOL's **Games** channel. There are also chat rooms for just about every game you can play. One task isn't enough room to show you how to play all these games, but you can learn to play one game: Slingo. Played with from one to ten members, this online game is fun and easy for everyone.

Begin

1 Choose Games

Make sure that you're signed on to **AOL** and click the **Games** button on the left side of the **Welcome** window. (You can also click the **Channels** icon in the toolbar and choose **Games**.) The **AOL Games** window opens.

Click

2 Choose Game Shows Online

This window provides links to different types of games and game resources. For this task, click **Game Shows Online**. The **Welcome to Game Shows Online** window opens.

Click

3 Choose Slingo

Scroll through the list box at the top of the window to look at the available games. Double-click **Slingo** in the alphabetical list of games. The **Slingo** window opens.

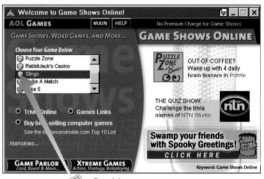

Double-click

4 Download Slingo

Click **Getting Started** to view a complete list of rules. When you're satisfied that you understand the game, click **Play Slingo**. You may be asked to verify the install location. Click **OK** to proceed with the download.

Click

6 The Rules of the Game

After you spin, numbers appear in the windows at the bottom of your screen. You have 30 seconds to click the numbers in the columns that match the numbers in the bottom windows. The player with the most points wins. Points are won by matching numbers; matching *all five numbers* in a row, column, or diagonal is called a Slingo.

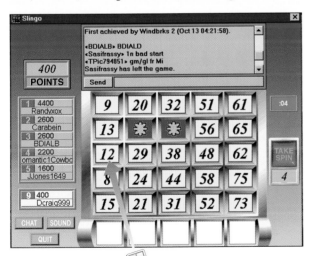

Click

End

5 Play Slingo

When the game starts, you'll take your spin when your **SPIN** button flashes red. Click the **SPIN** button, and you're on your way. You might find the game more exciting and tricky because you're playing with online opponents. (In other words, you're not playing with your hand-picked buddies at home.)

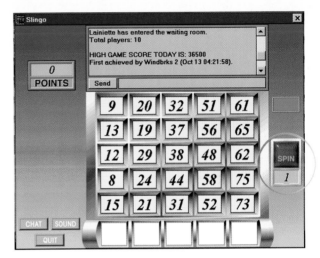

How-To Hints

Downloading Slingo Software

The first time you play Slingo, you have to download some software to your computer. It just takes a few minutes, and AOL automatically installs it for you so that you're ready to go. Click **OK** to confirm the directory.

For What It's Worth

A match is worth 200 points. If you use a Joker, it is also worth 200 points. Gold coins are worth 1,000 points. A spin with a devil reduces your current points by half (unless you're saved by a cherub, in which case the cherub saves your points). Each Slingo is worth 1,000 points, and you can have 12 possible Slingos. Bonus points are awarded if you get all 12 in fewer that 20 spins. Spins 17 through 20 *cost* you points. If you have a free spin, you have the option of when to use it.

Glossary

A

address book   An electronic address book in which you can store the screen names and Internet email addresses of everyone you need to send email to. This way you can select the addresses, instead of typing them in from scratch, each time you want to send email.

America Online (AOL)   An online service that provides access to the Internet as well as specialized services and information. America Online also supplies the software that enables you to connect to the America Online service.

AOL Live!   An AOL area that produces live events such as conversations with authors, actors, and various celebrities. Unlike chat rooms, which allow only a limited number of participants, **AOL Live!** events are held in virtual "auditoriums" that can accommodate thousands of members.

AOL Mail   A tool that enables you to check your AOL mail using Microsoft Internet Explorer.

attachment   A file—text, graphic, or other—that you "attach" to a piece of email and transfer to a friend or co-worker using email. To use the attached file, the recipient needs to save it and open it in the program with which it was created.

Automatic AOL   An AOL feature that lets you schedule tasks or events that you want to happen automatically. You can use Automatic AOL to send and receive mail, to send and receive newsgroup postings, and to download files. One of the main purposes of Automatic AOL is to limit your online time, both to keep expenses down (if you don't have unlimited access) and to keep your phone line free.

B–C

blind carbon copy   A copy of an email message you can send to someone without the other message recipients being aware of this fact.

browser   *See* Web browser.

Buddy Lists   Lists of family, friends, or colleagues who are on AOL. The Buddy List window indicates when someone in one of your Buddy Lists is online. This way, you can send him or her an Instant Message or join him or her in a chat room.

cache   An area on your computer's hard disk in which Web pages you've visited recently are stored. That way, if you return to a Web page you've already visited, it is retrieved quickly from the cache rather than downloaded from the Web (which takes more time).

carbon copy   A copy of an email message you can send to someone without listing them as a primary recipient. You might "CC" someone to keep that person posted about a situation, without necessarily requesting him or her to take any action.

channels Content areas within AOL. AOL provides over a dozen channels on subjects ranging from personal finance to travel to news to computers. (The word *channels* may have different meanings in different contexts. For example, in Windows, channels are Web sites to which you can subscribe to have them send content to you.)

chat room An area of AOL in which you can have real-time conversations with a group of other AOL members. Chat rooms can sometimes be fun and informative. The conversations that occur in other chat rooms can be immature or offensive.

compression program A program that enables you to condense files to a smaller size so that they're easier to transfer with a disk or modem. You can also compress multiple files into a single compressed file, which makes them not only smaller but more manageable. To use compressed files again, you must uncompress them, which you can often do with the same file you used to compress them in the first place. (PKZip and WinZip are two of the most common compression programs.)

D–E

dialog box A screen that typically requires you to provide additional information, such as the name of the file you want to print or open.

directory A subsection of a hard disk; sometimes also called a *folder*.

download To transfer a file from another computer (often on AOL or the Internet) to your own computer.

Download Manager An AOL feature that helps you download files. You can choose a large number of files to download, and then instruct the Download Manager to download them all at once, maybe in the evening or on the weekend so that your computer won't be tied up when you would otherwise want to use it.

downloadable files Files you can transfer from the Internet to your computer and then use from your local hard drive.

email Electronic mail. Messages that you send electronically and that wind up in the recipient's electronic mail box. Formerly, email messages consisted only of text, but now you can send images and more.

email address The address that you use to send someone an email message. If you're sending mail to someone else on AOL, you can just use his or her screen name. If you're sending email to someone on the Internet, you need to send to an address such as `janeblow@location.com`.

F

FAQ (Frequently Asked Questions) A compiled list of questions that users commonly ask, along with their answers. A FAQ is typically a great place to look for information if you're trying to inform yourself about a new area or subject. In a newsgroup, it's good manners to read the FAQ before you start asking questions left and right (many of your questions have probably been answered plenty of times before).

Favorite Places AOL areas or Web sites that you mark so that you can return to them more easily. To save an area as a Favorite Place, just click the heart icon in the window's upper-right corner.

file transfer To move files from another location (such as the Internet) to your computer so that you can use the files. Also called *download*.

freeware Software, typically that you find online, that you can download and use for free.

FTP An acronym for File Transfer Protocol. FTP is widely used to transfer files from one computer to another on the Internet.

FTP site A location on the Internet from which you can download files by using FTP.

G–H

group name The name assigned to a group of email addresses. When you send email to this name, email is sent to all the people in the group. As just one example, you could create a group called **Family** and assign to it all the email addresses for your parents, siblings, children, cousins, and so forth. Then if you had a special family announcement, you could send it to everyone at once just by sending it to the group name **Family**.

history trail   A list that you can drop down from the AOL toolbar to display and go to the 25 AOL areas or Web sites you've visited most recently.

home page   The Web page that's set to appear first thing when you start your browser (also sometimes called a *start page*). *Home page* can also mean the page that someone has created for himself or herself on the World Wide Web.

HTML   Hypertext markup language. The language used to create Web pages. HTML is not particularly difficult, but if you use a tool such as Personal Publisher, you can create Web pages much as you would create a word-processed document, without having to learn any HTML at all.

hyperlink   *See* link.

hypertext   A snazzy name for text that you can read in a variety of sequences because it contains hyperlinks leading to other material. Most Web pages consist of hypertext; you can read as you like and click links to jump to other areas, where you can continue reading. In other words, you're not limited to reading in a linear fashion, from start to finish.

I

image map   An image that serves as a link—that is, you click it to travel to another location on the Web. (Typically, when you point to an image map, your mouse pointer changes into a pointing hand.)

Instant Message (IM)   Private messages that you can send to other AOL members who happen to be online at the same time as you are. These messages appear almost instantly on the recipient's screen. You can use Instant Messages to carry on a real-time conversation with another

AOL member who is online. If someone is on one of your Buddy Lists, you're informed when he or she comes online and can easily send him or her an Instant Message. (Non-AOL members who install special software can also trade Instant Messages with AOL members.)

interest profile   A profile you set up that indicates what your interests are. Based on this profile, AOL delivers you periodic emails telling you about AOL sites you might want to visit.

Internet   An enormous, global network of computers that are interconnected so that people around the world can use them to communicate and share information. AOL gives you access to the Internet. The World Wide Web is one of the most well-known and popular aspects of the Internet.

Internet service provider (ISP)   A service to which you can subscribe that enables you to access the Internet. ISPs typically provide you with Internet access but don't supply extra content on top of that.

J–L

Java   A popular Web programming language that works for all platforms. That is, whether someone uses a Mac, a PC, or some other platform, he or she will be able to view Web objects that were programmed using Java.

keyword   A word you can type to go directly to a specific area of AOL, without having to travel there using links.

link   Text (usually underlined and displayed in a different color) or an image on a Web page that you can click to jump to another location on the Web—whether another place on the same page, another page in the same Web site, or another site altogether. (Sometimes also called *hypertext links*, or *hyperlinks*.)

Lobby   An AOL chat room without any area of focus. Typically, the Lobby is crowded with unsupervised teenagers with raging hormones who don't have anything better to do. If you're in the mood to chat and you fall into some other category, you may want to hunt for a more topic-specific room. (Even there, the conversations may have a tendency to deteriorate.)

M

mailbox The place where your electronic mail is stored.

master account The AOL account name that you originally signed on to AOL with. You can also set up subaccounts under the master account for use, for example, by different members of your family. However, there are certain activities, such as setting up subaccounts, that you can only do from the master account.

member profile A personal information form that you can fill out so that other AOL members can find out about where you live, your hobbies, your occupation, and so forth.

menu A drop-down list of options from which you can choose. Menus usually appear when you click an option in the menu bar. Menus also appear when you click certain AOL toolbar icons.

menu bar The list of options, usually arranged horizontally across the top of the screen, that you can click to display a related menu of choices.

message board The electronic equivalent of the message boards you often find in libraries and laundromats. They are areas of AOL in which you can post messages related to a specific topic and, hopefully, receive responses from other AOL members.

modem Modulator/demodulator—a piece of equipment for translating computer information into data that can be transmitted over phone lines.

N

netiquette Informal rules of behavior for the Internet. Most of these rules are common sense, such as "don't flame other users" (send inflammatory and abusive messages), "don't send spam" (unsolicited commercial messages), "don't SHOUT," and so forth.

network A group of computers connected together so that they can share programs, data, and peripherals such as printers.

news profile A profile you set up that indicates what type of news you're interested in. Based on this profile, AOL delivers news articles to your mailbox.

newsgroups Topic-specific areas in which you can post messages and receive replies. Newsgroups are much like AOL message boards but are not confined to AOL members. Unlike chat rooms, newsgroup conversations do not happen in real time.

O

offline help Help with AOL that you can get while you are not signed on. This form of help is less extensive and less current than online help, but can be very useful if you're not able to get online.

online help Help with AOL that you can get while you are signed on. This help is much more comprehensive and up-to-date than offline help.

online service A company, such as AOL, that provides both access to the Internet and specialized services and information.

P

parental controls AOL features that parents can use to limit their children's access to various aspects of AOL and the Internet.

password A confidential word or set of characters that you use to access your AOL account and that keeps your account secure from others. When choosing a password, be sure to specify one that you'll remember but that no one else is likely to guess. (It's safer *not* to write down your password, so pick something you won't forget.)

path An indication of the drive and directory or directories in which a file resides. For example, `C:\AOL\download\filename.doc` indicates that the file **filename.doc** is on drive C, in the **download** subdirectory of the AOL directory.

Personal Filing Cabinet   An AOL tool that lets you save and organize all your email—both mail that you receive and mail that you send. Each screen name has a separate Personal Filing Cabinet associated with it.

Personal Publisher   An AOL tool that makes it easy for you to create your own Web page.

preferences   Settings that let you customize AOL's behavior to suit your needs. For example, you can set preferences to determine whom you can receive email from, whether a user with a particular screen name can access chat rooms, and much more.

Q–S

QuickStart   An area of AOL that provides several tools—such as a five-minute tour of AOL and **AOL FastFacts** (formerly the **Best of AOL**)—for getting you up-to-speed in AOL quickly.

screen name   The unique name of three to sixteen characters that you use to identify yourself to and access AOL. (If you want, you can set up multiple screen names in AOL.) If someone is sending you mail from the Internet rather than AOL, he or she needs to use your screen name followed by **@aol.com**. (For example, if your screen name is **jsmith**, someone on AOL can simply send mail to **jsmith**; someone on the Internet has to send mail to **jsmith@aol.com**.)

shareware   Software, often found online, that you can typically download and use for free for a trial period. After that, you're supposed to pay for the software, but it is usually quite inexpensive.

shortcut key   A key combination you can use to execute a command without going through the menu system. Often shortcuts are listed to the right of the command name in the menu. For example, you can issue the **Print** command by pressing **Ctrl+P** instead of choosing **Print** from the **File** menu.

sign off   To disconnect your modem and make your phone line available for regular phone calls again.

sign on   To connect to America Online so that you can use all of its features. When you sign on, your modem dials and connects to AOL; at this point, your phone line becomes unavailable to receive regular phone calls.

signature file   A file—typically containing your name and possibly your address and phone or fax number—that you can construct and then insert into your email messages. You can create multiple signatures per screen name.

software libraries   Specialized file collections into which AOL's downloadable files are organized. Software libraries, which are found in many AOL areas, are usually indicated by buttons or list box items that display a stack of floppy disks.

spam   Unsolicited email. Sending out spam violates the rules of netiquette. Unfortunately, spam is a fact of life on today's Internet.

start page   *See* home page.

subaccount   An AOL account name underneath the master account with which you originally signed on to AOL.

subscribe   To join a newsgroup or to add it to your AOL **Read My Newsgroups** list.

T–V

threaded   When the original message and any replies to it are grouped together in message boards or newsgroups, they are said to be threaded.

toolbar   A series of icons located directly beneath the AOL menu bar. You can use these icons to get around AOL and the Internet.

upload   To transfer a file from your computer to some other computer, possibly on AOL or the Internet.

URL (uniform resource locator)   A Web address. A typical URL reads something like **http://www.sierraclub.org**. If you know a Web site's

URL, you can travel to the site directly (by typing the URL into the **Go** text box and pressing **Enter** or clicking **Go**), rather than by clicking a series of links.

virus A program that "infects" files you may download from AOL or the Internet. Viruses interfere with the normal operations of your computer in some way. Some viruses are fairly benign, only playing silly tricks such as displaying messages on your screen. Other viruses can be massively destructive, doing things such as erasing the contents of your hard disk.

W–Z

Web browser A program that enables you to view and use the Internet and the World Wide Web. Microsoft's Internet Explorer and Netscape Navigator are two of the most popular browsers at the moment.

Web page A particular document on the World Wide Web.

Web site A collection of Web pages associated with a particular person, business, or organization.

wildcard A character that stands in for one or more characters, often in a search operation. The * wildcard character acts as a substitute for one or more characters, while the **?** character stands in for only a single character. As an example, a search for **?ore** would find *bore*, *core*, *fore*, *gore*, *lore*, *more*, and so on, but would *not* turn up *store*. A search for ***ore** would turn up all the preceding words, plus *store*, *galore*, and *snore*.

wizard A special program that guides you step by step through a process, such as an installation procedure.

World Wide Web A user-friendly area of the Internet, in which graphics, animations, and sounds abound, and you can navigate easily just by clicking links with your mouse.

Index

numbers

access

adding, 9

changing, 9

selecting, 8-9

registration, 10

toll-free, offline help, 25-27

O

obscene language (chat), reporting, 167

offline

Download Manager, 41

email, composing, 45

Help, 24

toolbar icons, available, 21

online, viewing buddies, 95

online communities (Lifestyles channel), 213

online games, Kids Only software, 219

Online Help, 27

defined, 230

starting, 26

online services, defined, 230

online shopping, 208

CDs, 207

checking out, 209

product categories, 208

security, 209

shopping bags, 209

store listing, 208

online shorthand, 109

online time, checking, 151

opening

Address Book, 84

downloaded files, 83

Edit menu, 16

email mailboxes, 72

File menu, 16

files, attachments, 82

Help menu, 17

Instant Message window, 96

Interest Profiles, 52

messages, Message Boards, 103

Newsgroups folder, Personal Filing Cabinet, 49

People Connection, 120

Personal Filing Cabinet, 48, 79

Quickstart, 28

Sign Off menu, 17

Sign On menu, 17

Windows menu, 16

options

Edit menu, 16

File menu, 16

installation, selecting, 6

Windows menu, 16

ordering personalized gifts, You've Got Pictures, 67

organizing Favorites, 59

outgoing mail, sending, AOL Automatic, 45

owning a business. See WorkPlace channel

P

parental controls

blocked features, 155

categories, selecting, 149

chat rooms, 154-155

defined, 230

email, 156-157

Instant Message, 158

neighborhood watch, 166-167

newsgroups, 160-161

saving, 155

Web, 159

password-protecting, Personal Filing Cabinet, 49

passwords

changing, 152-153

defined, 230

multiple screen names, 149

registration, 10

saving, 92

selecting, 11

storing, 11, 13, 153

paths, defined, 230

payment methods, AOL, 10

PC Upload Center window, 42

people, locating (White Pages), 133

People toolbar icon, 21

People Connection

chat schedules, 120

opening, 120

periodicals, reading, 173

Perks toolbar icon, 21

Permanently Delete button, 77

Personal Filing Cabinet

defined, 231

Download Manager, 48

files

compacting, 49

deleting, 49

folders

adding, 49

finding, 49

mail, reading, 48

Newsgroups folder, opening, 49

opening, 48, 79

password protecting, 49

Personal Filing Cabinet Preferences, setting, 33

Personal Finance channel, 176-177

mutual funds, researching, 178-179

portfolios, creating, 177

stocks, tracking, 176-177

Personal Publisher, defined, 231

personalized gifts (You've Got Pictures), ordering, 67

Pet Rescue Clearinghouse, 203

Pets area (Interests channel), 202-203

phones services, identifying, 8

photo albums, creating, 67

photo developers, finding, 66

pictures

emailing, 67

retrieving, 14

saving, 67

viewing, 66

playing

Slingo, 224-225

sounds, chat rooms, 117

portfolios (financial), creating, 177

postings

Automatic AOL

retrieving, 45

sending, 45

message boards, 104-105, 217

newsgroups, 137

signatures, setting, 105

preferences

changing, 33

chat

editing, 116

notifications, 117

viewing, 117

defined, 231

Download Manager, setting, 41

email

master accounts, 79

setting, 78

subaccounts, 79

My AOL, 32-33

newsgroups, setting, 139

Personal Filing Cabinet, setting, 33

Preferences window, setting, 32

Web, setting, 126

Preferences window, setting preferences, 32

previewing

channels, 171

Web pages, 129

pricing plans, viewing, 63

Print toolbar icon, 20

printing

email, 72

maps, 145

recipes, 201

private chat rooms, entering, 119